NEW DIRECTIONS FOR CHILD DEVELOPMENT

William Damon, *Brown University*
EDITOR-IN CHIEF

Children, Youth, and Suicide: Developmental Perspectives

Gil G. Noam
Harvard University
and McLean Hospital

Sophie Borst
Harvard University
and McLean Hospital

EDITORS

Number 64, Summer 1994

JOSSEY-BASS PUBLISHERS
San Francisco

CHILDREN, YOUTH, AND SUICIDE: DEVELOPMENTAL PERSPECTIVES
Gil G. Noam, Sophie Borst (eds.)
New Directions for Child Development, no. 64
William Damon, Editor-in-Chief

Microfilm copies of issues and articles are available in 16mm and 35mm, as well as microfiche in 105mm, through University Microfilms Inc., 300 North Zeeb Road, Ann Arbor, Michigan 48106-1346.

LC 85-644581   ISSN 0195-2269   ISBN 0-7879-9960-1

NEW DIRECTIONS FOR CHILD DEVELOPMENT is part of The Jossey-Bass Education Series and is published quarterly by Jossey-Bass Inc., Publishers, 350 Sansome Street, San Francisco, California 94104-1342 (publication number USPS 494-090). Second-class postage paid at San Francisco, California, and at additional mailing offices. POSTMASTER: Send address changes to Jossey-Bass Inc., Publishers, 350 Sansome Street, San Francisco, California 94104-1342.

EDITORIAL CORRESPONDENCE should be sent to the Editor-in-Chief, William Damon, Department of Education, Box 1938, Brown University, Providence, Rhode Island 02912.

Cover photograph by Wernher Krutein/PHOTOVAULT © 1990.

Manufactured in the United States of America. Nearly all Jossey-Bass books, jackets, and periodicals are printed on recycled paper that contains at least 50 percent recycled waste, including 10 percent postconsumer waste. Many of our materials are also printed with vegetable-based inks; during the printing process these inks emit fewer volatile organic compounds (VOCs) than petroleum-based inks. VOCs contribute to the formation of smog.

CONTENTS

Editors' Notes

Albert Camus, the French existentialist, once wrote that the only interesting philosophical question worth asking is suicide. To this day, his idea remains intriguing even if he may have been wrong. Suicide poses the question of free will at the border between life and death. Maybe Camus exaggerated in order to provoke his readers, for there are certainly other essential philosophical questions that remain worth studying besides suicide. But most philosophical questions involve the question of suicide. How do we live a moral life? How do we value life? What role does government play to protect life and to interfere in a citizen's decision to end it? Is living out one's biological life course a choice or a duty?

Increasingly, the public and professionals recognize that suicidality is at the core of moral and ethical problems in medicine, psychology, psychiatry, and education. In popular magazines and scholarly journals, the questions posed concern how justified someone is in making a rational choice about suicide and how this choice differs from someone else who commits suicide in a situation that is only seemingly irresolvable and thus "irrational." When we apply these questions to children and adolescents, the problems of suicide and suicidal behavior are even more protracted. In what way does age or legal status play a role in our evaluation of suicide, especially when it is known that suicidal behavior is often related to conflicts with parents?

However, suicidality in children and adolescents is not just an interesting academic issue relevant to legal and medical ethics. It is also a frightening phenomenon on a steady rise for decades. Over the past few decades, rates of both completed and attempted suicides have rapidly increased among adolescents (Diekstra and Moritz, 1987; World Health Organization, 1989), constituting the second leading cause of death among adolescents in the United States (National Center for Health Statistics, 1989).

This fact, though not well understood, has created a great deal of concern among policymakers, health care professionals, educators, and community workers. The alarming increase has resulted in a wealth of studies on risk and protective factors in suicidal children and adolescents. Many risk factors have been delineated by now, including sociodemographic, age, gender, psychiatric (for example, affective disorder, propensity toward aggressive and impulsive behavior), psychosocial (for example, parental loss and family disruption, unwanted pregnancy, being a friend or family member of a suicide victim), and genetic and biological variables (for example, neurotransmitter imbalances) (see Blumenthal, 1990, for an overview).

Despite this growing body of knowledge supported by many international research efforts, prediction of suicidal behavior remains extremely difficult, with a high probability of error (Alcohol, Drug Abuse, and Mental Health Adminis-

1

tration, 1989). Furthermore, we still lack a clear picture of the antecedents, causes, and consequences of suicidal behavior in childhood and adolescence.

The need for a developmental understanding becomes evident even on a phenomenological level when we take into account the incidence of suicide attempts and completions in children and adolescents. Although suicidal behaviors are relatively rare under the age of twelve, the prevalence increases considerably during middle and late adolescence (for example, Carlson and Cantwell, 1982; Kienhorst, De Wilde, Diekstra, and Wolters, 1990). Similarly, completed suicide is extremely rare before the age of twelve, even though suicidal ideation is not uncommon (for example, Pfeffer, 1986; Stillion, McDowell, and May, 1989).

It has been observed that suicidal behavior may increase during adolescence because, in part, of the rapid cognitive, emotional, and social maturation taking place. This maturation includes the capacity for formal operational thinking as well as new skills for self-observation. Suicide always has an evaluative-cognitive component, manifested in an interpretation of life as not worth living, and is accompanied by a set of serious negative emotions (Borst and Noam, 1993). However, this exciting potential of integrating our expanding knowledge about normative development and child and adolescent psychopathology and suicidality still needs to yield fruit.

Despite the complexity of the many developmental processes involved, most previous developmental studies have emphasized chronological age as a critical variable. However, age is a very crude indicator when it comes to a variety of deeper psychological processes such as cognition, emotion, social development, and coping styles (for example, Noam, 1992). Under normal conditions, many of these processes are, of course, correlated with age, but it is precisely in the area of dysfunction and conflict where these associations often break down. For those reasons, it is important to gain greater insights into the underlying developmental processes that are involved in child and adolescent suicidal behavior. It was, in fact, this need for insights that provided us with the central motivation to create this volume.

Our initiative was furthered by the need for dialogue between developmental psychologists and clinical researchers. In the case of children and adolescents, it is hard to imagine how one can make any progress in understanding suicide without reflecting on the strengths and weaknesses of the crucial developmental points that mark childhood. This effort is massive, requiring the expertise of developmental researchers, clinical practitioners as well as child and adolescence psychiatrists, psychologists, social workers, nurses, educators, and so on. Fortunately, our knowledge has advanced far enough and the integrative research endeavors have progressed sufficiently to provide us with more than merely plans, goals, or speculation. We therefore chose to bring together a group of scientists at a point when a variety of specific developmental approaches to suicide have already emerged, but still before the developmental research of child and adolescent suicide has grown to a point where an edited volume would only provide a loose collection of very advanced lines of research.

In this volume, *Children, Youth, and Suicide: Developmental Perspectives*, we have assembled a group of distinguished psychologists and psychiatrists with the hope that rigid disciplinary boundaries can be avoided in the study of suicide. The different expertise of personality psychologists, developmentalists, as well as psychiatric researchers is apparent throughout this volume. While most contributors are from the United States, we have tried to introduce the work of Canadian and European colleagues.

Obviously, not one underlying developmental process is responsible for suicidality. Too many cognitive, emotional, and behavioral systems are involved and too many types of suicidality (for example, suicidal attempts versus completed suicides) exist for one set of processes to account for this diversity. But we worked with this group of authors to specify those developmental capacities and vulnerabilities that could be linked most closely to suicidality.

In Chapter One, McDowell and Stillion present a suicide trajectory model that is based on their excellent literature review pertaining to suicidality in different age groups. They rely on developmental theorists such as Piaget and Erikson to understand the risk factors for attempted and completed suicide for two age groups, namely, children and adolescents.

In Chapter Two, Döbert and Nunner-Winkler present a model influenced by the moral psychologist Lawrence Kohlberg, introducing levels of conceptualizations and reasoning about suicide. Examples of developmental levels pertaining to suicide come from their larger empirical study in identity formation and youth crisis. In addition, they create an important link between a cognitive-conceptual understanding of suicide and reasons for suicide with coping resources.

In Chapter Three, we explore the relation of social-cognitive development and suicidal behavior in psychiatrically hospitalized adolescents. We introduce a general suicide typology supported by systematic research and exemplified by qualitative interview data.

In Chapter Four, Chandler focuses on the experience of continuity of self as a significant line of development that, when disrupted, can lead to serious suicidal behavior. Under normal conditions, Chandler argues, cognitive complexity and "persistence-through-time" experiences develop hand-in-hand. His interviews with children and adolescents have shown that this synchrony is not present in suicidal subjects.

Harter and Marold have studied the developmental line of self-competence and, recently, have supplemented the child competence scales with very promising depression research. In Chapter Five, they address the relationship between self-competence, depression, and suicidality.

In Chapter Six, Carlson, Asarnow, and Orbach present their findings of an empirical study on developmental aspects of suicidal behavior. They compared a group of psychiatrically hospitalized children with a group of young adolescents who were mentally retarded or developmentally delayed on their knowledge of death and suicide. They found that depression scores, IQ, knowledge of the finality of death, exposure to suicidal behavior, and knowledge of suicidal methods were different for suicidal and nonsuicidal psychiatrically hospitalized children and developmentally delayed adolescents, and that these factors in turn impacted differently, depending on age and development.

Finally, in Chapter Seven, Pfeffer discusses the contributions in this volume by demonstrating the significance of a developmental perspective on suicide research and suicide prevention. She reminds us of the complex interplay of risk factors and development.

Taken together, these chapters provide an important step in combining meaningful theorizing, empirical exploration, and clinical observations on child and adolescent suicide. This volume contributes to a productive search for underlying causes of suicidality in children and adolescents. It also presents a meaningful picture of the relationship between development and suicidality. It is our hope that this increased knowledge will eventually help reverse the increasing rate of suicide that afflicts our young.

In closing, we thank a number of institutions, foundations, and people who made this project possible. Gil Noam worked on this book during a productive year at the Institute for Advanced Studies in Berlin. The American Suicide Foundation in New York has provided us with funds for our own research and through an institutional grant has supported the interdisciplinary Harvard Suicide Research Committee. Dr. Herbert Hendin, its president, and Dr. Alan Lipschitz, the associate director for research, could not have been more supportive. Many individuals at Harvard Medical School, the Human Development and Psychology Program of the Harvard Graduate School of Education, McLean Hospital, and the University of Leiden have been extremely helpful intellectually, clinically, and administratively in ensuring that we could create the work presented in this volume. We are especially thankful to Drs. Joseph Coyle, Steven Mirin, Silvio Onesti, Mona Bennett, Susan Villani, Philip Treffers, Rene Diekstra, Kurt Fischer, and Robert Selman. We also thank Karen Hoffman for her excellent editorial help and Barbara Panza for her continual secretarial support for more than a decade. We dedicate this volume to the children, adolescents, and families who participated in the studies presented here.

Gil G. Noam
Sophie Borst
Editors

References

Alcohol, Drug Abuse, and Mental Health Administration. *Report of the Secretary's Task Force on Youth Suicide.*DHHS Publication No. ADM 89-1621. Washington, D.C.: Government Printing Office, 1989.

Blumenthal, S. "An Overview and Synopsis of Risk Factors, Assessment, and Treatment of Suicidal Patients Over the Life Cycle." In S. Blumenthal and D. J. Kupfer (eds.), *Suicide Over the Life Cycle: Risk Factors, Assessment, and Treatment.*Washington, D.C.: American Psychiatric Press, 1990.

Borst, S., and Noam, G. G. "Developmental Psychopathology in Suicidal and Non-Suicidal Adolescent Girls." *Journal of the American Academy of Child and Adolescent Psychiatry,*1993, *32,* 501–508.

Carlson, G., and Cantwell, D. "Suicidal Behavior and Depression in Children and Adolescents." *Journal of the American Academy of Child and Adolescent Psychiatry,* 1982, *21,* 361–368.

Diekstra, R., and Moritz, B. "Suicidal Behavior Among Adolescents: An Overview." In R. Diekstra and K. Hawton (eds.), *Suicide in Adolescents.* Dordrecht, Netherlands: Martinus Nijhoff, 1987.

Kienhorst, C., De Wilde, E., Diekstra, R., and Wolters, W. "Characteristics of Suicide Attempters in a Population-Based Sample of Dutch Adolescents." *British Journal of Psychiatry,* 1990, *156,* 243–248.

National Center for Health Statistics. *Vital Statistics of the United States: 1987.* Rockville, Md.: National Center for Health Statistics, 1989.

Noam, G. G. "Development as the Aim of Clinical Intervention." *Development and Psychopathology,* 1992, *4,* 679–696.

Pfeffer, C. R. *The Suicidal Child.* New York: Guilford, 1986.

Stillion, J. M., McDowell, E. E., and May, J. *Suicide Across the Life Span. Premature Exits.* New York: Hemisphere, 1989.

World Health Organization. *1988 World Health Statistics Annual.* Geneva, Switzerland: World Health Organization, 1989.

GIL G. NOAM is associate professor of psychology/psychiatry and education at Harvard Medical School and the Human Development and Psychology Program, Harvard Graduate School of Education. He is also director of the Hall-Mercer Laboratory of Developmental Psychology and Developmental Psychopathology at Harvard Medical School and McLean Hospital, Belmont, Massachusetts.

SOPHIE BORST is clinical psychologist at Curium Academic Center for Child and Adolescent Psychiatry, The Netherlands. She is also research associate at the Hall-Mercer Laboratory of Developmental Psychology and Developmental Psychopathology at Harvard Medical School and McLean Hospital.

A suicide trajectory model is applied to explain commonalities and age differences in risk factors affecting suicide across the life span.

Suicide Across the Phases of Life

Eugene E. McDowell, Judith M. Stillion

Suicide is a universal human behavior. History and literature are replete with examples of suicides, from the death of Socrates to the recently produced play *Night Mother*. Philosophers have debated the merits of suicide since the time of the ancient Greeks, and modern medical ethicists are presently discussing the wisdom of assisting suicide among terminally ill patients. Sociologists, following Durkheim's ([1897] 1951) seminal work, have attempted to explain the ways in which suicide is a product of social and cultural influences. Psychologists have examined suicide from the perspective of the individual, probing for the roots of suicidal tendencies and attempting to establish treatments that speak to individual hopelessness. Within the past two decades, the medical establishment has become a major player in the arena, armed with drugs that are prescribed to treat suicidal depression rooted in the biology of the brain. Until very recently, however, there has been little attention to the developmental aspects of suicidal behavior.

The purpose of this chapter is to examine the subject of suicide from a developmental perspective, with special emphasis on youth suicide. Developmental psychologists believe that behavior is dependent, at least in part, on the maturity of individuals as they interact with their environments. Maturity is composed of both biological and psychological maturation. Six-year-olds cannot think or react like sixteen-year-olds, in part because they lack the life experience of sixteen-year-olds and in part because they have not acquired the physical structures to think like sixteen-year-olds. Until the last third of the twentieth century, psychologists generally recognized potent developmental forces influencing behavior from birth through maturity, but little attention was paid to development beyond age eighteen. Today, the field of life-span psychology has blossomed, bringing with it a multitude of studies of predictable changes throughout young and middle adulthood and old age (Gould, 1978;

Levinson and others, 1978; Vaillant, 1977; Sheehy, 1976). The preponderance of data from these studies indicate that examining behavior from a life-span perspective adds a dimension of understanding that cannot be attained in any other way. In fact, the behavior of individuals cannot be understood apart from the problems, crises, challenges, and events that are central to the age and developmental stage that individuals are currently experiencing.

Suicidal behavior is especially well suited to examination from a developmental perspective because of the documented, near-universal age differences in suicide. To illustrate these differences, suicide rates in thirteen developed countries are listed in Table 1.1. While the suicide rates differ from country to country and from male to female, one of the most impressive differences in the table is the age differences in suicide. Every country shows an increase in the suicide rate across the life span. That increase tends to be more dramatic for males than for females, increasing as much as seven times from the teen years to old age in the case of French males. Females show a similar, if less impressive, increase in the rate of suicide across the life span.

There are historical trends in suicide among different age groups. These trends are particularly impressive among children and adolescents in the United States. The death rates for suicide among children ages ten to fourteen increased two and one-half times (.6 per 100,000 to 1.5) between 1970 and 1986, while those for young people age fifteen to nineteen almost doubled (5.9 per 100,000 to 10.2) (U.S. Bureau of the Census, 1990, p. 86). Furthermore, the suicide rate for young people ages fifteen to twenty-four rose sharply during the decades of the 1950s, 1960s, and 1970s until it reached and exceeded the overall suicide rate for the total population, while the suicide rate for older groups remained relatively stable (Stillion, McDowell, and May, 1989).

Most of the demographic data concerning self-destructive behavior in different age groups pertain to completed suicide. Less is known about age-related changes in attempted suicide, and we are aware of no studies addressing suicide ideation from a life-span perspective. It is widely believed that the suicide attempt-completion ratio is inversely related to age. Young people attempt suicide more often and complete it less often, whereas older people attempt less and complete it more often. Weissman (1974) estimated that people under thirty years of age account for 50 percent of all suicide attempts, but the most recent demographic data show that this age group accounts for less than 33 percent of the suicide completions. Although the most widely accepted suicide attempt-completion ratio is 8:1 for all ages, the adolescent ratio of attempts to completions has been estimated to be as high as 200:1 (Angle, O'Brien, and McIntire, 1983), while the corresponding ratio for those over age sixty-five has been approximated to be 4:1 (McIntosh, 1985).

In this chapter, we provide a general model that attempts to organize what is known about suicide into major categories. The model can serve as a template for understanding suicide at different ages. Our assumption is that by examining the major categories of risk factors that promote suicide against the backdrop of what is happening developmentally to people of different ages, we can gain a better understanding of suicide in all age groups.

Table 1.1. Suicide Rates for Selected Countries, by Sex and Age Group

Sex and Age	United States 1986	Australia 1986	Austria 198?	Canada 1986	Denmark 1986	France 1986	Italy 1985	Japan 1987	Nether- lands 1986	Poland 1987	Sweden[a] 1986	United Kingdom[b] 1987	West Germany 1987
Male													
Total[c]	20.6	19.1	40.1	22.8	35.6	32.9	12.2	25.6	13.9	22.3	27.1	11.6	26.7
15–24 years old	21.7	21.1	29.3	26.9	16.5	16.0	5.2	11.6	8.1	17.8	19.5	9.3	17.6
25–34 years old	25.5	28.3	42.9	32.0	33.2	43.2	9.2	23.7	15.2	30.6	29.4	14.6	24.3
35–44 years old	23.0	23.5	44.8	28.5	50.6	38.1	10.1	29.4	15.3	32.3	33.8	14.6	27.7
45–54 years old	24.4	23.1	54.9	28.1	54.3	46.3	14.8	45.5	19.6	38.5	38.8	15.0	35.2
55–64 years old	26.7	24.6	48.5	27.6	62.2	47.8	22.0	40.5	22.6	35.0	36.1	17.8	37.5
65–74 years old	35.5	27.1	68.1	28.4	52.9	63.5	33.7	42.1	25.5	29.9	39.3	15.8	43.9
75 years old and over	56.0	36.8	125.2	36.3	65.5	121.3	50.0	73.0	42.8	33.2	48.0	20.0	77.2
Female													
Total[c]	5.4	5.6	15.7	6.4	19.9	12.9	4.7	13.8	8.2	4.7	10.1	4.5	11.8
15–24 years old	4.4	5.4	8.1	5.3	5.2	4.6	1.3	6.5	3.6	3.0	7.9	2.1	4.5
25–34 years old	5.9	6.3	10.7	7.5	14.0	10.1	2.7	9.9	9.1	5.7	11.0	3.8	7.8
35–44 years old	7.6	7.5	15.9	8.9	24.6	14.4	4.3	10.9	10.9	6.4	14.6	4.6	10.4
45–54 years old	8.8	10.8	16.8	11.4	36.7	20.2	5.9	16.9	13.6	8.0	15.4	7.6	15.6
55–64 years old	8.4	8.3	22.9	8.9	44.2	21.2	8.8	21.2	13.5	7.7	15.3	7.3	17.4
65–74 years old	7.3	7.6	33.8	9.2	29.3	25.4	11.8	31.1	12.5	7.7	12.7	8.1	23.2
75 years old and over	6.8	6.2	35.4	5.5	26.0	29.5	12.4	53.2	13.0	6.9	8.8	6.9	23.7

Note: Figures are rates per 100,000 population. They include deaths resulting from self-inflicted injuries. Except as noted, deaths were classified according to the ninth revision of *International Classification of Diseases (I.C.D.)*.

[a] Based on the eighth revision of I.C.D.
[b] England and Wales only.
[c] Includes other age groups not shown separately.

Sources: World Health Organization, 1989; U.S. Bureau of the Census, 1990, p. 838.

Suicide Trajectory Model

The suicide trajectory model, based on a review of the research and theoretical literature pertaining to suicide in different age groups (Stillion, McDowell, and May, 1989), is shown in Figure 1.1. This model suggests that there are four major categories of risk factors that contribute to suicidal behavior at every age: biological, psychological, cognitive, and environmental. As the arrows indicate, each of these categories of risk factors may directly influence suicidal ideation and may affect other categories of risk factors. For example, having a biological inclination toward depression can directly affect suicidal ideation and, at the same time, cause an individual to develop low self-esteem and to interpret environmental events selectively in a negative fashion. Likewise, poor environmental conditions, such as an abusive home, can elicit suicidal ideation and also may be a starting point for low self-esteem.

As seen in the suicide trajectory, suicidal ideation, which includes the making of specific suicide plans, is an essential phase in all but the most impulsive suicides. Suicidal ideation may manifest itself in warning signs. These

Figure 1.1. Suicide Trajectory Model

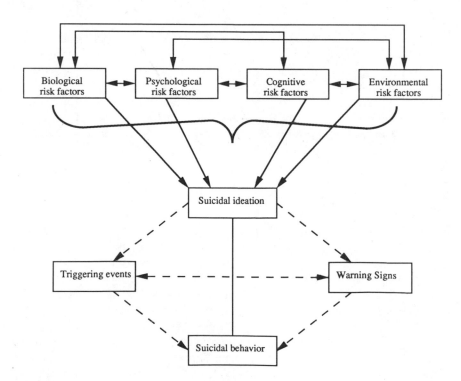

Source: Stillion, McDowell, and May, 1989, p. 240.

indications of impending suicide vary greatly in their obviousness, from vague and abstract references to death to specific threats and gestures. In many cases, however, after the suicide has been completed, people can retroactively point to warning signs. Warning signs may become more obvious after a triggering event that solidifies the suicide plan. Triggering events, like warning signs, are not universally present in suicidal behavior. However, the sometimes delicate balance between positives and negatives in a person's life may be destroyed by one more argument, one more failing grade, one final broken relationship—in short, any type of "last straw" triggering event.

For the remainder of this chapter, we utilize the suicide trajectory model in discussing research findings and theory concerning suicide across the life span. We discuss commonalities in the suicide trajectory model that apply to all age groups, as well as aspects that are idiosyncratic to two age groups: childhood (five to fourteen years old) and adolescence (fifteen to twenty-four years old). A summary of the commonalities and the childhood and adolescent age-group-specific aspects of the suicide trajectory is presented in Table 1.2. Because this volume focuses on youth suicide, we do not include aspects of suicidal behavior that are specific to older age groups (for applications of this model to adult age groups, see Stillion, McDowell, and May, 1989).

Commonalities in the Suicide Trajectory

Each risk factor listed in the first row of the suicide trajectory presented in Table 1.2 contains elements that transcend all ages, defining commonalities across the life span. In the biological category, for example, research has shown that there is a biological basis of depression that is age-irrelevant. The biological basis of depression is associated with low levels of several neurotransmitters, especially serotonin (Asberg, Nordstrom, and Traskman-Bendz, 1986; Banki and Arato, 1983). Recent findings show that the incidence of suicidal behavior in depressed and in nondepressed patients is related to low levels of the serotonin metabolite, 5-HIAA, and low levels of the dopamine metabolite, HVA (Asberg, 1991). In other words, the neurotransmitters, serotonin and dopamine, appear to influence suicidal behavior as well as depression.

Individuals differ in their genetic predispositions to develop crippling depression (Lester, 1986). Some people become significantly depressed with little or no environmental pressure, whereas others experience depression only under the most extreme stress. In an extensive review of the research literature on genetic factors in suicidal behavior, Roy (1991) reported findings from twin studies and adoption studies in the United States and Denmark that indicate both depression and suicide have significant hereditary components.

Another biological factor that predisposes individuals of all ages to suicide is maleness. This fact appears to be true across cultures and throughout history. Although it is impossible to ferret out the exact contributions of biological factors, such as testosterone level, and male socialization practices, which emphasize competence, self-reliance, and social isolation, males are

Table 1.2. Life-Cycle Commonalities and Age-Group-Specific Aspects of the Suicide Trajectory for Childhood and Adolescence

Age Group	Biological Risk Factors	Psychological Risk Factors	Cognitive Risk Factors	Environmental Risk Factors	Warning Signs	Triggering Events
Life-cycle commonalities	Depression Genetic factors Maleness	Depression Low self-esteem Helplessness Hopelessness	Rigidity of thought Selective abstraction Overgeneralization Inexact labeling	Negative family experiences Negative life events Presence of firearms	Verbal threats Previous suicide attempts	"Final straw" life event
Childhood (5–14 years old)	Impulsivity	Feelings of inferiority Expendable child syndrome	Immature views of death Concrete operational thinking	Abuse and neglect Inflexible family structure Unclear family member roles Parent conflict	Truancy Poor school performance Anxiety Sleep disturbance Aggression Low frustration tolerance Impulsiveness	Minor life events
Adolescence (15–24 years old)	Puberty Hormonal changes	Identity crisis Fluctuating mood states	Formal operational thinking Idealistic thinking Increased egocentrism Imaginary audience Illusion of invulnerability	Parent conflict Anomic family Drug or alcohol abuse Social isolation Poor peer relationships Population characteristics	Change in habits Self-mutilation Truancy Poor school performance Preparation for death	Failure experiences Problems with peers, parents, siblings, or opposite sex Suicides by peers or famous people

Source: Based on Stillion, McDowell, and May, 1989, p. 244.

more aggressive than females from birth onward, and they are more likely to turn that aggression on themselves.

Turning to psychological risk factors, depression and accompanying low self-esteem are important contributors to suicide in every age group (Borg and Stahl, 1982). Although we have stated that there is a biological component to most, if not all, severe depression, depression must also be discussed as a psychological risk factor. Depression tends to be perceived by those suffering from it as a psychological rather than a physiological syndrome; that is, depressed people talk more about their feelings than about their physiological symptoms. Furthermore, evidence exists that suicide risk is elevated when depression is coupled with feelings of hopelessness and helplessness (Topol and Reznikoff, 1982). In fact, level of hopelessness has been shown to be a stronger predictor of attempted suicide and completed suicide than is depression (Beck, Steer, Kovacs, and Garrison, 1985).

Turning to cognitive risk factors, evidence is accumulating that suicidal individuals tend to become more rigid and dichotomous in their thinking and to narrow their cognitive focus to suicide as the best and only answer to their current problems (Beck, 1967). These individuals also tend to use selective abstraction in recalling only negative episodes in their lives and ignoring the positive ones. They tend to overgeneralize from one event, such as a failed relationship, and assume that future relationships will turn out the same way. Inexact labeling, where suicidal individuals place on themselves negative labels that exclude positive attributes, is also often a part of suicidal cognition (Beck, Kovacs, and Weissman, 1979).

Completing the common risk factors across the life span are those that exist in the environment. Research clearly shows that negative family experiences increase the risk of suicide (Bock and Webber, 1972; Garfinkel, Froese, and Hood, 1982; Stephens, 1985). Abuses of all types and separations, whether brought about by death or divorce, are life stresses within the family that have been shown to be related to suicidal behavior. An accumulation of negative life events, especially those involving loss, tends to increase the probability of a suicidal response. Finally, there is growing evidence that the presence of the means of self-destruction, especially firearms, increases the likelihood of suicide in all age groups (Hudgens, 1983; Brent and others, 1988).

As shown in Table 1.2, there are commonalities also in the warning signs and triggering events that precede a suicidal act. Verbal threats are by far the most common suicide warning signs. People often tell others, in more or less subtle ways, about their suicide plans. The most lethal warning sign, however, is previous suicidal behavior. Farberow (1991) has reviewed a number of studies showing that prior self-destructive behavior (especially a suicide attempt) is a powerful predictor of later completed suicide for many age groups. As discussed earlier, suicides are sometimes preceded by final straw triggering events, which tip the balance between life and death for one who is already somewhat ambivalent about both.

While it is important to note the commonalities in the suicide trajectory, it is equally important from a developmental perspective to examine the differences that are related to age and developmental level. In the remainder of this chapter, we apply the template of the suicide trajectory to what is known about suicide in children and adolescents.

Childhood Suicide

As shown in Table 1.2, impulsivity is a risk factor that may increase the likelihood of suicidal behavior during the childhood and early adolescent years (ages five to fourteen). Children are more impulsive and violent in their suicidal behavior than any other age group (Joffee and Offord, 1983). They are more likely than older age groups to commit an impetuous self-destructive act such as jumping from a high place or running in front of a car, and they are less likely to engage in suicidal behavior that involves planning such as the hoarding and injesting of drugs (Kosky, 1983).

As indicated in Table 1.2, we believe that there may be a biological basis to the impulsivity that characterizes many child suicides, as has been shown to be the case for hyperactivity (Derryberry and Rothbart, 1984). It should be noted also, however, that Pfeffer's (1986) research has shown repeatedly that many suicidal children live in homes where impulsive self-destructive behavior is modeled frequently. Therefore, the impulsive nature of child suicide may reflect either biological or environmental risk factors, or an interaction of both.

It can be seen in Table 1.2 that there are two major psychological factors that increase children's risk of suicide. The first, which is explained in detail by Erikson (1980), is a sense of inferiority. Erikson pointed out that children need to develop feelings of confidence and positive self-regard, which he called a sense of industry. According to Erikson, children who fail to develop a sense of industry experience strong feelings of inferiority and develop poor self-concepts and low self-esteem. These children frequently act out in ways that confirm their low opinions of themselves and increase the likelihood that they will receive negative feedback from important people in their lives, thus instituting and perpetuating a downward spiral of ever-increasing feelings of inferiority and low self-esteem. Although there is no direct evidence that low self-esteem leads to suicidality in children, Pfeffer (1986) pointed out that the family systems of suicidal children produce negative self-concepts in addition to depression and hopelessness. Also, our research dealing with attitudes toward suicide has shown that children and adolescents with low self-esteem, as measured by the Tennessee Self-Concept Scale, agree more with all reasons for suicide than do others in their ages (Stillion, McDowell, and Shamblin, 1984).

The second psychological risk factor specific to childhood is the expendable child syndrome (Sabbath, 1969), which involves very low self-esteem in addition to other significant problems. The expendable child experiences loss of love in the most extreme form. Parents of these children communicate very low regard for, hostility toward, and even hatred of them on a daily basis. These children believe that they are unworthy and expendable and that their deaths will not matter to anyone. Patros and Shamoo (1989) presented case studies to illustrate how the expendable child syndrome may activate a wish to die. Sabbath (1969) believes that the expendable child often uses suicide to stop being a burden to a parent.

The cognitive risk factor most closely associated with childhood suicide is the immature view of death, which many children have (Nagy, 1948; Wass and Stillion, 1988). Young children do not realize that death is final and irreversible; they tend to view death as a temporary and reversible state. They expect to "wake up" and rejoin their grieving families after a brief time. Orbach and Glaubman (1979) found that even older children, who have more mature views of death, tend to regress in their understanding of the permanence and irreversibility of death when facing a suicidal crisis. Pfeffer's (1986) clinical work with suicidal children uncovered support for this position also. She described children in a suicidal crisis as manifesting "ego constriction" that leads to a regression in their thinking about death.

A second cognitive factor affecting child suicide is the rigidity associated with concrete operational thinking, which characterizes the mental processes of children between the ages of six and eleven (Piaget and Inhelder, 1969). Children in the concrete operations stage tend to view the world in black and white and are very poor hypothetical and abstract thinkers. They are unable to consider multiple outcomes in a problem situation, including the possibility that things might get better. Concrete operational thinking resembles in many ways the characteristically rigid thought patterns associated with suicide at later ages. Once these children reach the conclusion that suicide is the answer, other solutions receive very little attention.

Environmental factors that influence suicidal behavior in children are naturally centered in the family. There is growing evidence that suicidal children are often victims of child abuse and neglect (Pfeffer, 1991; Rosenthal and Rosenthal, 1984; Green, 1978). It is clear also that even when these children do not suffer outright abuse and neglect, their family environments are less healthy than those of other children. Pfeffer (1982) reported that the families of suicidal children tend to be inflexible and resistant to change. These families frequently lack clear role definitions for parents and children. Too often these children find themselves carrying adult responsibilities for younger siblings and sometimes for the parents.

In addition, the homes of suicidal children are often marked by high levels of turbulence. Crises of all types seem to occur more often in these families, and the incidence of spouse abuse, divorce, and separation is greater than usual among these families (Kosky, 1983; Orbach, Gross, and Glaubman, 1981). Finally, the parents of suicidal children are more likely than others to model self-destructive behaviors, which include suicide attempts.

Many of the risk factors that have been found to be associated with child suicide are related also to other childhood disturbances. For example, at least two studies have found child abuse to be a significant factor in the family histories of many psychologically disturbed children (Pfeffer, Conte, Plutchik, and Jerret, 1979, 1980). It may be, however, the particular combination of environmental risk factors, which includes abuse and neglect, inflexibility, unclear roles, conflict, and the modeling of suicidal behavior, that impacts uniquely on child suicide.

Warning signs in childhood include truancy and poor school performance (Lewis and others, 1988). Children may demonstrate depression differently from adults. Depressed children may manifest increased anxiety, sleep disturbance, aggressive behavior, low frustration tolerance, and poor impulse control (Patros and Shamoo, 1989). Triggering events for child suicide are often minor occurrences; a seemingly tiny incident may trigger a suicidal act.

Adolescent Suicide

With respect to the middle and late adolescent years (ages fifteen to twenty-four), Table 1.2 shows that the most prevalent biological risk factor for this age group is the onset of puberty, triggered by the increased production of hormones that bring about sexual maturation. The process of maturation occurs over a period of years, and its onset may occur any time between the preteen and midteen years. Whenever these biological changes occur, they add weight to the tumult of this age period, and, we believe, increase suicide risk. Although there is no direct evidence that the onset of puberty increases suicide risk, the suicide rate for the postpubescent age group is significantly higher than that for preteens.

In the category of psychological risk factors, the establishment of a sense of identity is a major developmental task of adolescence. As Erikson (1980) explained, teenagers who develop some consistent understanding of who they are and who they are becoming will have a foundation of competence in coping with the stresses of this period. In contrast, adolescents who struggle with their identities are less likely to develop the coping skills needed to deal effectively with these challenges. Another psychological risk factor is the fluctuation of mood states, which is experienced by all adolescents. Moodiness, which is partially rooted in biology, may be extreme, reflecting a significant amount of depression, which has been shown repeatedly to be associated with increased suicide risk in all age groups.

Adolescents are also undergoing rapid change in the cognitive realm. As teenagers become capable of formal operational thought, they begin to engage in hypothetical and abstract thinking for the first time (Piaget and Inhelder, 1969). Their hypothetical thinking capability often leads to the creation of idealized worlds, which do not, of course, correspond with reality. The result of this idealistic thinking, tinged with an egocentric sense of personal tragedy, is sometimes a great deal of disillusionment. Additionally, adolescents experience a renewed period of egocentrism, as they believe that they are the first ones to really understand the world from this new perspective. This egocentrism fuels their sense of performing for an imaginary audience and increases their feelings of self-consciousness, making small embarrassments seem like major traumas. Finally, adolescents have great difficulty accepting their own mortality. They often hold an illusion of invulnerability, which contributes to high risk taking among this age group (Elkind, 1967). Although there is no evidence of a direct relationship between enhanced disillusionment, self-consciousness, and risk taking and suicidality, we believe that these are risk factors that add to the perturbation of adolescence and affect vulnerability to suicide.

The literature is clear on environmental risk factors for suicide among adolescents. Many suicidal adolescents, like younger children, come from highly conflicted homes that are unresponsive to the young person's needs (Berman and Carroll, 1984; Pfeffer, 1991). There is a higher-than-average incidence of family dysfunction as evidenced by spouse abuse, alcoholism, and drug abuse among the parents of suicidal adolescents (Garfinkel, Froese, and Hood, 1982; Tishler, McKenry, and Morgan, 1981).

Farberow (1991) reviewed a number of studies showing that suicidal adolescents are often socially isolated, alienated individuals. Suicidal adolescents are likely to have poor peer relationships (Topol and Resnikoff, 1982). They are frequently nonjoiners and generally unpopular at school (Curran, 1987). Also, drug and alcohol abuse is frequently associated with adolescent suicidal behavior (Greuling and DeBlassie, 1980; McKenry, Tishler, and Kelly, 1983). Drugs are frequently used in suicide attempts (especially among teenage women), and alcohol is often taken as a prelude to a suicide act. Also, the risk of suicide is greater among adolescents who are heavy users of drugs and alcohol (Schuckit and Schuckit, 1991).

Holinger and Offer (1991) hypothesized that a major environmental influence on the rate of adolescent suicide is their representation in the general population. They predict that the suicide rate for adolescents will increase as this age group constitutes a larger percentage of the total population and will decrease as their relative numbers decline. They believe that larger numbers of adolescents increase competition for relatively fewer societal rewards (for example, class president, valedictorian, team captain) and result in more "failure" and lost self-esteem. Several studies have shown significant relationships between adolescent representation in the U.S. population and the suicide rate for this age group (Holinger, Offer, and Zola, 1988; Holinger and Offer, 1991). Predictably, the adolescent suicide rate peaked in 1977, when this age group's population representation reached its zenith, and both statistics have correspondingly declined since. The Holinger and Offer theory predicts that the adolescent suicide rate will begin to climb again in 1995 as this age group again claims a higher percentage of the total population.

Triggering events for adolescent suicide often seem trivial to adults. The previously mentioned egocentrism of this age group often inflates the importance of seemingly minor events such as failure experiences or problems with peers, parents, siblings, or the opposite sex (Spirito, Overholser, and Stark, 1989).

Two triggering events of special importance for this age group are suicides by peers and by famous people. It is well documented that adolescents have the highest vulnerability of any age group to cluster and copycat suicides (Davidson and Gould, 1991; Coleman, 1987; Gould and Shaffer, 1986). The suicides of peers and of famous people appear to have special modeling effects on adolescents. During the 1980s, highly publicized cluster suicides occurred in places as diverse as Plano, Texas; Westchester, New York; Omaha, Nebraska; and Bergenfield, New Jersey. In each of these situations, a single or group suicide served as a prelude to others in tragic episodes of adolescent conformity to powerful models. Although the real-life suicides of others do affect the adolescent suicide rate, the impact of televised fictional suicides is unclear. Several studies have produced conflicting and equivocal findings (Gould and Shaffer, 1986; Phillips and Paight, 1987; Steed and Range, 1989; Davidson and Gould, 1991).

As shown in Table 1.2, many of the warning signs of adolescent suicide differ from those of other age groups. Adolescents are more likely than others to show changes in their free-time habits and to mutilate themselves. Most troubled adolescents, including those who are suicidal, tend to perform poorly in school and to be truant frequently (Lewis and others, 1988). Finally, adolescents, more than any other age group, often broadcast their self-destructive plans with closure behaviors such as giving away prized possessions.

In summary, a review of the risk factors, warning signs, and triggering events for child and adolescent suicide shows both continuity and discontinuity between these two age groups. Actuarially, there is a continuum of increasing lethality reflected in the growing suicide rate from childhood and early adolescence (ages five to fourteen) to middle adolescence (ages fifteen to eighteen) to late adolescence (ages nineteen to twenty-four). Both children and adolescents who are at risk for suicide are more likely than other age groups to come from unsupportive, unhealthy, and anomic families marked by parent conflict and aggression. Both children and adolescents show warning signs such as poor school attendance and performance and the various subtle and not-so-subtle signs of depression. On the other hand, child and adolescent suicides are different phenomena in many ways. For example, a syndrome of impulsivity and hyperactivity may reflect a biological risk for suicide in children, while factors related to puberty are more important for adolescents. Psychologically, inferiority feelings and the expendable child syndrome loom large for suicidal children, while problems of identity and mood fluctuations are more important for adolescents. A child's immature view of death as reversible and temporary is a significant risk factor, while idealism, egocentrism, and the illusion of invulnerability are more important cognitive characteristics for adolescents. Finally, the environmental risk factors for child suicide are heavily rooted in family characteristics, while environmental factors for adolescents also include peer relationships and adolescent population characteristics. Triggering events for child suicide are seemingly minor life events. Adolescent suicide, in contrast, is more likely to be triggered by what appear to be significant failures or long-standing problems with family or peers. The suicides of peers or famous persons are especially powerful triggering events for adolescents.

Conclusion

In this chapter, we have presented a suicide trajectory model to explain commonalities and age-related differences in suicidal behavior. It is our hope that this model, with its four categories of risk factors and their relationships with suicidal ideation, warning signs, and triggering events, will be helpful in better understanding suicidal behavior of people in every phase of life.

This model of risk factors in suicide across the life span is built on developmental theories and empirical research on suicide in different age groups. We rely heavily on theorists such as Piaget and Erikson for help in understanding both commonalities and differences in suicidal behavior among various age groups. Clearly, more empirical evidence is needed in order to support or refute some of the theoretical assumptions in this model. For example, Erikson's theory predicts that the feelings of inferiority inherent to the expendable child syndrome make these children more vulnerable to suicide. However, there are no studies relating this syndrome directly to suicidality. A second problem with this model is that many of the risk factors associated with suicidality are also related to various types of emotional disturbances, especially in young people. For example, child abuse has been shown repeatedly to relate to both suicidal behavior in children and to various types of emotional disturbances. It is possible that suicidal behavior represents the extreme on a continuum that ranges from normal behavior to emotional disturbance to suicidal actions for all age groups. If this is so, then we would expect to find that negative life events are correlated with all types of emotional problems as well as with suicide. Finally, we cannot escape the fact that most of the research that must be relied on in investigating models such as ours is correlational in nature and, therefore, cannot uncover crisp and unequivocal cause-effect relationships. Clearly, we are dealing with very complex phenomena in trying to understand the commonalities and differences in suicide across the life span.

References

Angle, C. O., O'Brien, T., and McIntire, M. "Adolescent Self-Poisoning: A Nine-Year Follow-Up." *Developmental and Behavioral Pediatrics*, 1983, *4*, 83–87.

Asberg, M. "Neurotransmitter Monoamine Metabolites in the Cerebrospinal Fluid as Risk Factors for Suicidal Behavior." In L. Davidson and M. Linnoila (eds.), *Risk Factors for Youth Suicide*. New York: Hemisphere, 1991.

Asberg, M., Nordstrom, P., and Traskman-Bendz, L. "Cerebrospinal Fluid Studies in Suicide." *Annals of the New York Academy of Sciences*, 1986, *487*, 243–255.

Banki, C. M., and Arato, M. "Amine Metabolites, Neuroendocrine Findings, and Personality Dimensions as Correlates of Suicidal Behavior." *Psychiatry Research*, 1983, *10*, 253–261.

Beck, A. T. *Depression: Clinical, Experimental, and Theoretical Aspects.* New York: Hoeber, 1967.

Beck, A. T., Kovacs, M., and Weissman, A. "Assessment of Suicide Ideation." *Journal of Consulting and Clinical Psychology,* 1979, *47,* 343–352.

Beck, A. T., Steer, R. A., Kovacs, M., and Garrison, B. "Hopelessness and Eventual Suicide: A Ten-Year Perspective Study of Patients Hospitalized with Suicide Ideation." *American Journal of Psychiatry,* 1985, *142,* 559–563.

Berman, A. L., and Carroll, T. A. "Adolescent Suicide: A Critical Review." *Death Education,* 1984, *8,* 53–64.

Bock, E. W., and Webber, I. L. "Suicide Among the Elderly: Isolating Widowhood and Mitigating Alternatives." *Journal of Marriage and the Family,* 1972, *34,* 24–31.

Borg, S. E., and Stahl, M. "A Prospective Study of Suicides and Controls Among Psychiatric Patients." *Acta Psychiatrica Scandinavica,* 1982, *65,* 221–232.

Brent, D. A., Perper, J. A., Goldstein, C. E., Kolko, J. A., Allan, M. J., Allman, C. J., and Zelnak, J. P. "Risk Factors for Adolescent Suicide: A Comparison of Adolescent Suicide Victims with Suicidal Inpatients." *Archives of General Psychiatry,* 1988, *45,* 581–588.

Coleman, L. *Suicide Clusters.* Boston: Faber and Faber, 1987.

Curran, D. K. *Adolescent Suicidal Behavior.* New York: Hemisphere, 1987.

Davidson, L., and Gould, M. S. "Contagion as a Risk Factor for Youth Suicide." In L. Davidson and M. Linnoila (eds.), *Risk Factors for Youth Suicide.* New York: Hemisphere, 1991.

Derryberry, D., and Rothbart, M. K. "Emotion, Attention, and Temperament." In C. E. Izard, J. Kagan, and R. B. Zajonc (eds.), *Emotions, Cognition, and Behavior.* New York: Cambridge University Press, 1984.

Durkheim, E. *Suicide.* (J. A. Spaulding and G. Simpson, trans.) New York: Free Press, 1951. (Originally published 1897.)

Elkind, D. "Egocentrism in Adolescence." *Child Development,* 1967, *38,* 1025–1034.

Erikson, E. H. *Identity and the Life Cycle.* New York: Norton, 1980.

Farberow, N. L. "Preparatory and Prior Suicidal Behavior Factors." In L. Davidson and M. Linnoila (eds.), *Risk Factors for Youth Suicide.* New York: Hemisphere, 1991.

Garfinkel, B. D., Froese, A., and Hood, J. "Suicide Attempts in Children and Adolescents." *American Journal of Psychiatry,* 1982, *139,* 1257–1261.

Gould, M. S., and Shaffer, D. "The Impact of Suicide in Television Movies: Evidence for Imitation." *New England Journal of Medicine,* 1986, *315,* 690–694.

Gould, R. E. *Transformations: Growth and Change in Adult Life.* New York: Simon & Schuster, 1978.

Green, A. H. "Self-Destructive Behavior in Battered Children." *American Journal of Psychiatry,* 1978, *135,* 579–582.

Greuling, J., and DeBlassie, R. "Adolescent Suicide." *Adolescence,* 1980, *15,* 589–601.

Holinger, P. C., and Offer, D. "Sociodemographic, Epidemiologic, and Individual Attributes." In L. Davidson and M. Linnoila (eds.), *Risk Factors for Youth Suicide.* New York: Hemisphere, 1991.

Holinger, P. C., Offer, D., and Zola, M. A. "A Prediction Model of Suicide Among Youth." *Journal of Nervous and Mental Disease,* 1988, *176,* 275–279.

Hudgens, R. W. "Preventing Suicide." *New England Journal of Medicine,* 1983, *308,* 897–898.

Joffe, R. T., and Offord, D. R. "A Review: Suicidal Behavior in Childhood." *Canadian Journal of Psychiatry,* 1983, *28,* 57–63.

Kosky, R. "Childhood Suicidal Behavior." *Journal of Child Psychology and Psychiatry and Allied Disciplines,* 1983, *24,* 457–467.

Lester, D. "Genetics, Twin Studies, and Suicide." In R. Maris (ed.), *Biology of Suicide.* New York: Guilford, 1986.

Levinson, D. J., Darrow, C., Klein, E., Levinson, M., and McKee, B. *The Seasons of a Man's Life.* New York: Knopf, 1978.

Lewis, S. A., Johnson, J., Cohen, P., Garcia, M., and Velez, C. N. "Attempted Suicide in Youth: Its Relationship to School Achievement, Educational Goals, and Socioeconomic Status." *Journal of Abnormal Child Psychology,* 1988, *16,* 459–471.

McIntosh, J. L. "Suicide Among the Elderly: Levels and Trends." *American Journal of Orthopsychiatry*, 1985, *35*, 288–293.

McKenry, P. C., Tishler, C. L., and Kelly, C. "The Role of Drugs in Adolescent Suicide Attempts." *Suicide and Life-Threatening Behavior*, 1983, *13*, 166–175.

Nagy, M. "The Child's Theories Concerning Death." *Journal of Genetic Psychology*, 1948, *73*, 3–27.

Orbach, I., and Glaubman, H. "The Concept of Death and Suicidal Behavior in Young Children: Three Case Studies." *Journal of the American Academy of Child and Adolescent Psychiatry*, 1979, *18*, 668–678.

Orbach, I., Gross, Y., and Glaubman, H. "Some Common Characteristics of Latency-Age Suicidal Children: A Tentative Model Based on Case Study Analysis." *Suicide and Life-Threatening Behavior*, 1981, *11*, 180–190.

Patros, P. G., and Shamoo, T. K. *Depression and Suicide in Children and Adolescents*. Needham Heights, Mass.: Allyn & Bacon, 1989.

Pfeffer, C. R. "Interventions for Suicidal Children and Their Parents." *Suicide and Life-Threatening Behavior*, 1982, *12*, 240–248.

Pfeffer, C. R. *The Suicidal Child*. New York: Guilford, 1986.

Pfeffer, C. R. "Family Characteristics and Support Systems as Risk Factors for Youth Suicidal Behavior." In L. Davidson and M. Linnoila (eds.), *Risk Factors for Youth Suicide*. New York: Hemisphere, 1991.

Pfeffer, C. R., Conte, H. R., Plutchik, R., and Jerret, I. "Suicidal Behavior in Latency-Age Children: An Empirical Study." *Journal of the American Academy of Child and Adolescent Psychiatry*, 1979, *18*, 679–692.

Pfeffer, C. R., Conte, H. R., Plutchik, R., and Jerret, I. "Suicidal Behavior in Latency-Age Children: An Empirical Study of an Outpatient Population." *Journal of the American Academy of Child and Adolescent Psychiatry*, 1980, *19*, 703–710.

Phillips, D. P., and Paight, D. J. "The Impact of Televised Movies About Suicide: A Replicative Study." *New England Journal of Medicine*, 1987, *317*, 809–811.

Piaget, J., and Inhelder, B. *The Psychology of the Child*. New York: Basic Books, 1969.

Rosenthal, P. A., and Rosenthal, S. "Suicidal Behavior by Preschool Children." *American Journal of Psychiatry*, 1984, *141*, 520–525.

Roy, A. "Genetics and Suicidal Behavior." In L. Davidson and M. Linnoila (eds.), *Risk Factors for Youth Suicide*. New York: Hemisphere, 1991.

Sabbath, J. C. "The Suicidal Adolescent: The Expendable Child." *Journal of the American Academy of Child and Adolescent Psychiatry*, 1969, *8*, 272–289.

Schuckit, M. A., and Schuckit, J. J. "Substance Use and Abuse: A Risk Factor in Youth Suicide." In L. Davidson and M. Linnoila (eds.), *Risk Factors for Youth Suicide*. New York: Hemisphere, 1991.

Sheehy, G. *Passages: Predictable Crises of Adult Life*. New York: Dutton, 1976.

Spirito, A., Overholser, J., and Stark, L. J. "Common Problems and Coping Strategies, Part 2: Findings with Adolescent Suicide Attempts." *Journal of Abnormal Child Psychology*, 1989, *17*, 213–221.

Steed, K. K., and Range, L. M. "Does Television Induce Suicidal Contagion with Adolescents?" *Journal of Community Psychology*, 1989, *17*, 166–172.

Stephens, J. B. "Suicidal Women and Their Relationships with Husbands, Boyfriends, and Lovers." *Suicide and Life-Threatening Behavior*, 1985, *15*, 77–89.

Stillion, J. M., McDowell, E. E., and May, J. *Suicide Across the Life Span: Premature Exits*. New York: Hemisphere, 1989.

Stillion, J. M., McDowell, E. E., and Shamblin, J. B. "The Suicide Attitude Vignette Experience: A Method for Measuring Adolescent Attitudes Toward Suicide." *Death Education*, 1984, *8*, 65–80.

Tishler, C. L., McKenry, P. C., and Morgan, K. C. "Adolescent Suicide Attempts: Some Significant Factors." *Suicide and Life-Threatening Behavior*, 1981, *11*, 86–92.

Topol, P., and Reznikoff, M. "Perceived Peer and Family Relationships, Hopelessness, and Locus of Control as Factors in Adolescent Suicide Attempts." *Suicide and Life-Threatening Behavior,* 1982, *12,* 141–150.

U.S. Bureau of the Census. *Statistical Abstract of the United States: 1989.* (110th ed.) Washington, D.C.: Government Printing Office, 1990.

Vaillant, G. E. *Adaptation to Life.* Boston: Little, Brown, 1977.

Wass, H., and Stillion, J. M. "Death in the Lives of Children and Adolescents." In H. Wass, F. M. Berardo, and R. A. Neimeyer (eds.), *Dying: Facing the Facts.* New York: Hemisphere, 1988.

Weissman, M. M. "The Epidemiology of Suicide Attempts, 1960-1971." *Archives of General Psychiatry,* 1974, *30,* 737–746.

World Health Organization. *1988 World Health Statistics Annual.* Geneva, Switzerland: World Health Organization, 1989.

EUGENE E. MCDOWELL is director of the Graduate Center of the University of North Carolina, Asheville.

JUDITH M. STILLION is associate vice chancellor for academic affairs at Western Carolina University, Cullowhee, North Carolina.

A cognitive model of levels of conceptualization and reasoning about suicide is related to nonpsychiatric youth.

Commonsense Understandings About Suicide as a Resource for Coping with Suicidal Impulses

Rainer Döbert, Gertrud Nunner-Winkler

Everyday language outlines a negative image of a person committing suicide. Traditionally, a lack of understanding is merged with secularized remnants of the Judeo-Christian condemnation of suicide. A picture is painted where irrationality and illness are dominant. This stereotype is further supported by the tacit presuppositions of current psychological testing: Researchers make use of scales that are taken from clinical psychology and by this mere fact tend to subsume suicidality automatically under the category of the sick (Marttunen, Aru, Henriksson, and Lönnqvist, 1991; Jacobs, 1992). At the same time, suicide proneness is implicitly conceptualized as a stable personality disposition: One has to presuppose stability if one wants to identify and treat a suicidal person in time.

Yet, "rational" or situationally stress-induced suicides (for example, by a lonely, incurably ill elderly person or by an individual in a situation of acute unbearable pressure) show that a research strategy that exclusively focuses on pathological dispositions must fail. Admittedly, this type of research has produced repeatedly confirmed correlates of suicide such as depressiveness (Bewskow, 1990; Beckham, 1991; Duggan, Sham, Lee, and Murray, 1991; Pfeffer, 1992) or negative self-image and aggression. But by and large this research is afflicted by many contradictions (for a review, see Schmidtke and Schaller, 1981; Borst and Noam, 1989; Pfeffer, 1991).

There is a broad consensus that research on suicide can only be adequate if it starts from the assumption that there are different types of suicidal acts (contemplating, threatening, attempting, committing suicide) and suicidal motives and takes different external stressors into account (see Katschnig, Sint, and Fuchs-Robetin, 1981). Therefore, we do not have to deny, for instance, the relevance of theories that reconstruct suicide as affective and narcissistic disturbances originating in early childhood. Yet, in the following, we try the opposite strategy: We want to test the limits of a cognitive approach to understanding suicide and to coping with suicidal impulses. Our main argument holds that in early adolescence suicidal attempts may result from environmental stress impinging on cognitive resources that, as a normal fact of human development, are still inadequate. But under the impact of these experiences the cognitive schemas of the subject may be reorganized in such a way that new coping resources originate. From this new vantage point, the subject defines the same stressful situations that before seemed overwhelming as inadequate, illegitimate reasons for suicide. One way to get at these definitions of the situation is to reconstruct the commonsense suicide theories of adolescents of different ages and to spell out their coping implications. We suppose that suicide understanding is just one aspect of ego development that seems to follow a developmental logic. We give an outline of this logic in the next section. In constructing the specific definition of a suicidal situation, the subject draws on more general dimensions of ego development (time horizon, reflexivity, and so on), which in and of themselves have coping implications too.

In this chapter, we use data that we collected for different purposes. We were interested in the relationship between intensity and type of adolescent crises, development of moral consciousness, and identity formation. We interviewed 113 fourteen- to twenty-two-year-old male and female adolescents of different socioeconomic backgrounds. The questions concerning suicide were intended as one set of indicators for the intensity of crisis experience. We asked, "Why and in which situation do you think people consider suicide? Have you yourself ever considered suicide?" If yes, "Why, what was your situation then? Do you think there is an acceptable reason for suicide?" Subjects responded on the basis of their own experiences with suicide attempts (real-life situations) or on the basis of hearsay (hypothetical situations). The responses were used to develop a stage model of suicide understanding. Certainly, stage models are beridden with problems; but semantic fields are not continuums and they always comprise levels insofar as reflective processes are at work (Level n is reflected on from Level $n + 1$).

Stages of Commonsense Suicide Theories

We have spelled out the developmental logic of this stage model in more detail elsewhere in the context of a discussion of the place of content in structural theories (see Döbert and Nunner-Winkler, 1985a, 1985b). Suicide understanding seems to offer a good basis for a discussion of structure-content problems because formal sociocognitive resources seem not to suffice to understand suicide. We give here only a short summary of the stages and add for each stage an analysis of its coping implications.

STAGE 1: *Momentary external incidents*

This type of suicide theory is exemplified by the following statements:

INTERVIEWER: Why do you think people commit suicide?
SUBJECT 77: Mostly because of problems with friends or with parents, because of school, or often also because of grades and such things.

Typical for responses at this stage is that the subjects on the whole are referring to momentary difficulties experienced by suicides in their social milieu. They feel no need to spell out underlying motives, since these seem so trivial anyhow: Problems give rise to frustrations and these explain the suicide. Explanations at this level are inadequate. No attempt is made to deal with the explanatory problem even in purely formal terms. At one time or another everybody has to cope with the kinds of problems mentioned, but most people do not commit suicide. An analysis of this type of explanation in terms of perspective taking proves that there are structural similarities to Selman's (Selman and Byrne, 1974) Stage 0 (that is, egocentric role taking as the inability to distinguish between a subjective interpretation and what is believed to be an objective description of a situation). The fact that any interpretation of a situation depends on the perspective taken is not, at least explicitly, acknowledged. In these suicide explanations the actor does not explicitly participate in the definition of the situation; instead, suicide is explained exclusively in terms of the objective givens.

Coping implications. At this stage, the subject operates with such a narrow definition of the situation that no coping options are visible. With perspective taking the subject also lacks the ability to situate a crisis in a broader social context or a wider time horizon. Thus, he or she cannot relativize a present experience as a particular subjective perception but instead sees it as a reflection of an objective situation from which there is no escape. Also, the subject is fixated on the present so that the possibility of changes in the future does not enter his or her mind. Thus, coping implications of suicide understanding at this stage are by and large negative.

STAGE 2: *Momentary external incidents in empty subjective perspective*

Again, we begin with an example for this stage:

SUBJECT 87: If they have problems that they can't cope with, when it seems there's nothing they can do anymore.
INTERVIEWER: What kind of problems are you thinking of, for example?
SUBJECT 87: Well, different kinds of problems, unhappiness in love, or problems at school or on the job.

Here the same objective triggering factors are invoked as at Stage 1, but these incidents no longer seem to be regarded as adequate explanations. The interviewees understand that the problems referred to may not be experienced as utterly unsolvable by all persons and need not per se lead to suicide: It is the situation viewed from a certain perspective that is experienced as hopeless. On the whole, this seems to match Selman's Stage 1 (that is, subjective role taking as the ability to understand that people think and feel differently because their situations and information differ). However, the cognitive advance is purely formal and that is why we call it "empty subjective perspective." It is recognized that stressful circumstances and standard motives alone do not provide a sufficient explanation, but no other substantive motives are cited and the gap is filled by tautological truisms (hopeless situation, problems they cannot cope with anymore) that express an awareness of the strangeness of suicide as such. A substantive elucidation, however, is not yet possible.

Coping implications: Even though subjects at this stage do not understand and cannot substantiate the perspective of the suicide, the mere fact of introducing perspectivity has an important coping implication: In seeing suicidal thoughts as a correlate of a particular perspective, the unavoidability of suicide is overcome and alternatives may come to be seen as possible.

STAGE 3: *Subject-constituted incidents in a social context and with an extended time horizon*

The cognitive advances of this stage are seen in the following example:

SUBJECT 4: Adolescents, maybe, because they are being pressed too hard to achieve in school or something like that, and maybe they are afraid to bring their report cards home, they're afraid because they have bad grades and their parents have kept on telling them the whole year, "Don't you come home with bad grades." Or if, for example, a boy has a fight with his girl or if maybe he can't even get to first base with a girl. Or else if grown-ups, for instance, lose their job and they are afraid. Say a man, who loses his job, he may be afraid that his wife wouldn't want him anymore, or if he doesn't know how to take care of his family.

INTERVIEWER: Do you find any of the reasons you have listed understandable?

SUBJECT 4: No, I don't. I think one should always first think about problems like that, and then see if they cannot be settled by talking them out. So that maybe young people with bad grades or with problems with their parents or on the job could perhaps find a solution by talking about it. Because most of the time suicide is just an act committed in the heat of the moment.

Obviously, the incidents referred to by subjects at lower levels appear here as well: bad grades, unemployment, a fight with a friend. But there is a new element as well: The specific incidents are no longer seen as objective givens but are reflected on in terms of the subject's perceptions, expectations, experiences, and dispositions; they are related to standards specific to the different life spheres and are placed within a wider time horizon. Now it is no longer just bad grades but being afraid (a disposition) of coming home with bad grades when the parents (an explication of the social context) have for the whole school year (a time horizon, the first idea of the processslike nature of the growth of despair) put their child under pressure. Similarly, the momentary fight with a girlfriend is associated with the general fear of never "getting to first base" with any girl. Concepts such as achievement pressure and setbacks or failure on the job, which replace the earlier formulations (problems, difficulties, troubles with the family, school, and job), either contain one's life plans (setbacks) or one's own standards (failure at school and achievement pressure). Unlike the explanations of lower levels, these concepts incorporate the subject's perspective into the very definition of the incidents and thus do more justice to the formal explanatory problem: Only those who have invested "segments" of their personalities into the life sphere of school will react to bad grades with suicide because they have internalized achievement standards.

Nevertheless, there remains a still-obscure part in suicide understanding: After all, it must be possible to find some sort of solution for such partial problems. Subject 79 articulated this uneasy feeling in stating, "Girlfriend gone, no job, those are not reasons I can accept." The feeling that there is an obscure portion at this stage typically manifests itself in the conception of suicide as a panic or heat-of-passion action. This conception results from substantive new experiences in adolescence that put one's own emotions and moods into perspective. Adolescents are often subject to sudden swings of mood, and awareness of such emotional cycles constitutes a conception of a rhythmical course of time in which a depressive phase may be followed by a good time.

Coping implications: The widening of the time horizon allows per se a distancing from the immediate suffering, but on this stage it is supplemented by the concrete experience that a down is usually followed by an up again. For this reason momentary external incidents no longer qualify as adequate reasons for suicide, that is, one copes with panic reactions through devaluation. Subject 27 illustrates this point nicely:

SUBJECT 27: Actually, it is stupid to commit suicide. After all, life keeps going on. What I mean is, sure there are things that make you feel low, but I think the saying "time will heal all wounds" is really true, because in the end that is what really happens. You may be badly depressed for the moment, but I think it is really stupid to go ahead and kill yourself, because in the end there is always some solution.

INTERVIEWER: Have you ever thought about suicide?

SUBJECT 27: Yes. But I don't think I would have the courage to do it. I have felt depressed sometimes or down, but then things get better again and in the end some solution could always be found; it always takes some time, I know that, but so far I have always found some way of coping with problems and I think it is always like that, and that is why I really think that suicide is a panic action.

Furthermore, since the motives cited for suicide are still bound to specific spheres of life, an escape is always possible by redirecting one's emotional commitments to other segments of life (for example, if one's career fails, maybe satisfaction can be drawn from family life). Also, the subject mobilizes the social context in order either to directly address the problem or else to find support in dealing with it.

STAGE 4: *Decline of situational incidents in favor of more specific motivational constellations*

At Stage 4, motives are conceptualized in a more diffuse and encompassing way: One feels "different," "inferior," "not needed anymore." If incidents are mentioned at all, they are presented as incidents that do not adequately explain human behavior because they are interchangeable and acquire significance only within a specific motivational context. The mentioning of incidents at this level has the function of leading to problems that affect the person as a whole, over different life spheres and over time. Suicide theories now focus primarily on the subject, whose general state of mind or plans of life are considered to be the decisive factor. At Stage 4, the person as a whole is so deeply afflicted (for example, despairing) that a basis for overcoming critical situations or moods is no longer available. Also, the motivational constellation focused on at Stage 4 no longer allows for a simple cyclical conception of time (there will be another up). The following themes and motives are specific for this stage: social isolation, feelings of inferiority, despair, and the processlike nature of self-destruction. The following subject provides a good illustration of reasoning at this stage:

SUBJECT 13: Yes, if they are very isolated and feel that there is no one they could turn to.
INTERVIEWER: Is there any reason you find acceptable?
SUBJECT 13: Yes, if you, well if you resolve to do something and work very hard to bring it off, and then it fails awfully and this thing you've worked so hard for fails due to some stupid coincidence. Or, if you feel that you have been left alone and you then withdraw yourself into isolation and cannot find a way out of it anymore, I think this is also a reason to commit suicide.

The motives and themes that Subject 13 mentions (social and self-generated isolation, failure of life planning) allow a deeper understanding of suicide. Now it becomes understandable why a situation would appear hopeless, and in what respect suicide is therefore more than merely a panic action. It does, after all, make quite a difference whether a person (as at Stage 1) has concrete problems on the job, whether a person (as at Stage 3) believes he or she will be a complete failure in his or her profession, or whether the person comes to feel generally inferior once and for all (because the idea of individual development in the life course seems still to be beyond reach).

Coping implications: Suicide understanding at this stage makes suicide seem more unavoidable than at the stages before. This seems counter to our claim that the development of suicide theories increases coping resources. Yet, it is to be noted that the range of legitimate motives for suicide is considerably reduced. The motive constellations characteristic of the former stages are rejected as insufficient, childish reasons for suicide: Problems within one sphere of life can be compensated for by satisfactions in others, age-typical conflicts can be looked through as such and relativized within a life-span view. (For example, Subject 19 said, "I can't imagine committing suicide, after all, I'm still so young, and if anything goes wrong—goodness—now you're nine-teen and you've got so much time left, many things can change.") Yet, those encompassing and complex motives that do pass the test of adequacy render suicide a more compelling option, because the person as a whole is affected.

STAGE 5: *Deepened conception of motives and multifactorial explanations*

Only very few of the interviewees responded so that they could unequiv-ocally be assigned to Stage 5. Hence, the description of Stage 5, even more than the descriptions of preceding stages, must be viewed as provisional. On the whole, the explanations produced are indeed more complex: Motives may be deepened; objective, historical, and social preconditions may be discussed; the consequences of a suicide for the social milieu are recognized, and the processlike nature of the suicidal act is more clearly conceptualized. It was also our impression that at this level the judgmental dimensions of understanding, explaining, and evaluating are more clearly differentiated.

SUBJECT 1: I believe that in our time people have lost track of things, or let me put it this way: as compared to the way of life people knew, say in the last century, modern times have meant a rupture so great and rapid that people feel they have been torn out of a life context and thrown into circumstances in which even now they are not yet settled, nor have they achieved a mea-sure of stability so that they could either alone or in a group deal with this situation, and that because of this, what they do, is simply to give up and say "that is no longer meaningful to me." Too many things are moving too quickly, and many people are not even aware that they are letting their life slip through their fingers, and only when it is too late do they realize "I have not accomplished anything yet, everything has been futile," and then they break down and may even commit suicide.

INTERVIEWER: Could you imagine that someone might have an acceptable rea-son for committing suicide?

SUBJECT 1: In most cases, I condemn suicide, although I can understand it. It does not get anywhere, I mean, we cannot all of us commit suicide and that is that. The problems remain and suicide does not solve them but may, on the contrary, raise even more problems to the relatives. I'd say it's rather irre-sponsible.

Meaninglessness is one of the central topics at that stage. True, formulations such as "everything has become meaningless" were used also by interviewees at previous stages. At lower levels they were used tautologically, taking the form of truisms, and in these cases the significance of meaninglessness is almost identical with the suicidal act. At Stage 4, the concept of meaninglessness is already given some content: As the suicide must on the basis of his or her personality structure experience his or her situation as hopeless, any life activity becomes meaningless (in the sense of useless). Only at Stage 5 is the concept of the meaning of life connected to the idea of embedding one's biography in a more comprehensive social or meaning context, transcending the individual. Meaninglessness here no longer consists of the futility of particular actions but rather of the absence of good reasons for one's own existence and conduct of life. This is clearly illustrated by Subject 1, who points to the need for biographical integration so that "life does not slip through one's fingers," that is, fall into disconnected, isolated actions. This interpretation of the problem of meaning shows that the individual transcends even the person as a whole and grasps larger frameworks within which the person as a whole can be situated.

This extension of the orientation space also manifests itself in a widening of the overall social field within which subjects localize suicide. The individual no longer is the sole cause but is seen as the product of a historical-social constellation that increases the probability of suicide (Subject 1: rapid social changes; Subject 26: decadence of a society that has reached its saturation point; Subject 102: lack of creativity in production-line work, overstimulation, and compulsive consumption). Nonetheless, subjects at Stage 5 do not simply reduce the individual to a product of existing conditions; rather, they are looking for a multifactorial explanation of suicide, which would answer problems left unsolved by lower-stage theories. Suicide also is no longer seen as a self-contained act of a single individual; rather, its impact on the social milieu is perceived (Subject 1: problems for the family).

On the whole it may be said that Stage 5 suicide theories connect objective causal factors with subjective motivational factors so that the phenomenon of suicide is more adequately grasped. This better understanding does not, however, prejudge the evaluation of suicide. At Stage 5, a clearer distinction is made between descriptive and prescriptive statements. Whereas at previous stages the question concerning the acceptability of suicide was often answered in terms of understandability, it is now answered clearly as a question of the justifiability of suicide.

Coping implications: The cognitive resources at this stage not only allow a better understanding of suicide but also engender new forms of distancing from "immature" suicide motives. The difference between understanding and justification defines a vantage point from which to reject one's own suicidal impulses. The same effect derives also from an expansion of the orientation space of the individual: When consequences for others are taken into account, one may conclude that suicide is "irresponsible." Inasmuch as the meaning of life is no longer conceived as something objectively given but as a task to be actively mastered by the individual, it does not seem adequate anymore to simply declare life as such as meaningless. Suicide can be viewed as flight. Also, the integrating of societal causes and conditions for suicide not only serves to render the incomprehensible aspect of suicide comprehensible but also may allow an objectivation of and distancing from suicidal impulses: One does not want to see oneself as a mere reflex of societal forces.

General Trends of the Stage Model

Those familiar with Loevinger's, Selman's, and Kohlberg's respective theories of ego, sociocognitive, and moral development will easily recognize that—tentative as the model still is—the well-known trends of structural research in this domain reemerge: The subjects orient first to the external situation, focus increasingly on the role of the subject, and finally integrate both; the schematization and concepts that the subjects use are increasingly generalized (concrete types of situations, various life spheres, global society); time horizon expands and becomes saturated with experience (hic et nunc, cycles, biographically irreversible time, historical time); actor schematizations are individualized and become less stereotypical; the psychological understanding of motives is deepened and their genesis is beginning to be reconstructed in terms of social structural conditions. This latter trend implies that monofactorial explanations are substituted by multifactorial ones. At the same time the formal explanatory problem (Why suicide?) is more adequately grasped. At Stage 1, all persons faced with problems and troubles are regarded as suicide-prone. At Stage 2, the group of potential suicides is narrowed: Only individuals who experience such problems in a particular way are held to be potential suicides. At Stage 3, the particular nature of this experience is concretized. At Stage 4, the inevitability of such experiences is made plausible (since the personality system as a whole is affected and means of compensation are not available). Finally, at Stage 5, the genesis of a typical Stage 4 motivational constellation is explained (for example, by recourse to rapid social change).

Over the stages the explanations achieve greater adequacy in that the group of potential suicides is increasingly narrowed down, and motives are differentiated and individualized. This becomes possible because later stages integrate increasingly more aspects of the life world, which are then available for explanation. Thus, the sequence seems to tap on development.

Validating the Model

Given that the construction of the above model was a by-product in the process of operationalizing the construct of adolescence crisis, it is not a surprise that restrictions are to be noted; interviewing did not in all cases go into sufficient depth. In the answers, motivational and cognitive factors may be somewhat confounded; subjects who rejected the very idea of suicide may have performed below their general level of ego development. Stage 5 may need a thorough reanalysis—in our sample, there were too few cases. In future investigations, it may prove helpful to confront subjects with hypothetical life situations depicting a person more or less justifiably considering suicide. Such systematic analyses might allow us to clearly disentangle issues of the evaluation and understanding of suicide and individual suicide proneness.

One more point warrants mention: We had the impression that although we were clinically untrained, we were able to identify subjects at high suicidal risk on the basis of their reactions to those few questions we posed. Indicative was the way in which these subjects described situations or motives leading up to suicide, betraying intimate knowledge of the situation of despair beyond their blunt responses to the question "Have you ever considered suicide yourself?" Thus, these rather simple questions might even be developed into a diagnostic instrument of use even to nonclinicians (like teachers). It is to be noted, however, that we posed these questions in the course of a lengthy interview after a trustful relationship between interviewer and subject had (in most cases) been established.

Despite the methodological shortcomings noted above, there is some evidence for the validity of the stage model presented. As Table 2.1 shows, suicide understanding correlates—as one would expect on theoretical grounds —with age and socioeconomic background, operationalized in terms of education level. One would also expect intrafamilial milieus to differ in the degree to which they foster interpersonal understanding. To test this assumption, we checked the relative frequency of subjects who scored one stage above or, respectively, below the suicide understanding of their age-mates in families with different styles of parent conflict solution. Subjects were presented with lists of twenty different prototypical reactions in conflicts and asked to select the five most typical of their fathers, their mothers, or both (for example, "my mother/father slams the door/runs away/gives in/stops talking about the problem at hand/yells at the partner/cries, starts drinking").

As Table 2.2 shows, mature subjects tend to come predominantly from families for which symmetric conflict solution is typical; immature subjects come from asymmetric (either father- or mother-dominated) families (alpha = .005) (for more details on this family typology, see Döbert and Nunner-

Table 2.1. Level of Suicide Theory as a Function of Age and Education

| | Education Level | | |
Age	Low	Medium	High
14–15 years old	1.9	2.1	2.8
16–17 years old	2.6	3.2	4.3
18 years old and over	3.0	3.6	3.7

**Table 2.2. Level of Suicide Understanding as a Function
of Parent Styles of Conflict Solution**

Level of Suicide Understanding	Parent Conflict-Solving Styles		Preference	
	Symmetric (percentage)	Asymmetric (percentage)	Coping (ø = 3.0)	Defense (ø = 1.8)
Above average (N = 25)	.68	.23	3.5	1.4
Below average (N = 13)	.22	.77	2.2	2.2

Winkler, 1983). This result is plausible insofar as it is only in the case of open and symmetrical conflict resolution that both partners have a chance to articulate their own needs and motives and that both are bound to take the needs of the other into account. Since commonsense suicide theories are based precisely on an understanding of the motives involved, the correlation found can almost be considered a logical relationship.

In addition to this indirect fostering effect provided by a favorable family setting, there is also a direct path toward greater maturity resulting from living through and mastering personal crises. This path was exemplified in two ways. First, subjects who had attempted to commit suicide showed a higher (on the average, half a stage) level of suicide understanding than did subjects who had never contemplated suicide, even though they usually came from family settings that were unfavorable for ego development (that is, rejecting, scornful, restrictive, authoritarian mothers and/or fathers). Their high understanding of suicide can count as an additional piece of evidence for construct validity: The specific experience of being tempted to commit suicide prompts intensive and serious thinking, which advances the individual's understanding of suicide. This path toward maturity is obviously ridden by an ambivalence, which may explain the discrepancy between our interpretation and those of Noam and others that higher stages produce more internalized disorders (depression) and thus greater vulnerability to suicide. Subjects in this group experienced more crises and had been endangered more seriously than other subjects. But they "made it" and used their experiences as opportunities for growth. When we recruited the sample, we looked for "normal" adolescents. Others in similar circumstances may have failed, and they might then have shown up in clinical samples.

Also, subjects with an intense adolescent crisis (operationalized by questions concerning the meaning of life, attitude change, self-worth, alienation, conflict with authorities, and so on) were overrepresented in the group of subjects with an above-average level of suicide understanding (about 40 percent versus 10 percent in the general sample). Second birth implies thorough working through of given orientations, including deviant impulses and conventions. Given that a differentiated understanding of suicide can be seen as an aspect of general ego development, it is not surprising that the level of suicide understanding was correlated also with defense or coping preferences (measures are defined in Döbert and Nunner-Winkler, 1980).

Table 2.2 shows that high defensiveness, that is, a pronounced tendency to distort reality in conflict situations, goes together with a below-average level of suicide understanding, and an above-average level of suicide understanding correlates with a definite preference for coping strategies, that is, a high ability to stick to rational definitions of the situation even when put under stress (see Haan, 1974).

In sum, despite the tentativeness of the theoretical interpretations and despite certain deficiencies in data collection, a consistent and meaningful pattern of interrelations between levels of suicide understanding and other variables emerged. This pattern gives some validation to the stage model presented.

Coping with Suicidal Impulses

In the total sample of 113 adolescents, 49 never had considered suicide and 80 percent of those clearly condemned suicide; 27 had thought about suicide in the abstract and about half of them condemned suicide; 22 had seriously considered and 11 had attempted suicide, and the majority of these two groups judged suicide as legitimate. These data show that suicidal thoughts are a reality for many adolescents. Subjects who had seriously considered suicide had lived under worse conditions: More often they came from broken homes, had aversive relationships with their parents, and more often had to cope with biographical ruptures (such as change of residence and change of school).

Already in describing the stage model we have tried to derive coping implications from the stage-specific suicide conceptions. In the following discussion, we test whether these assumptions hold. To do this, we look at the way in which subjects handled their own suicidal impulses. Information on this topic is incomplete and does not warrant statistical analysis. Thus, we only illustratively make use of qualitative data. These allow us to distinguish three types of resources that foster coping with suicidal impulses: (1) general motivational resources, which are stage-independent; (2) general dimensions of ego development (ego resources), which are also manifested in suicide understanding; and (3) commonsense suicide theories as a specific interpretation of a concrete type of behavior.

We begin with motivational resources. The literature abounds with factors such as self-worth, locus of control, mastery, and basic trust that are considered important variables in predicting immunity from suicidal risks. From our theoretical perspective, their function is mainly negative: They work as filters blocking any serious consideration of committing suicide in stressful situations because "There's always a way out" (Subject 103), "There are always people who can help, you only need to turn to them" (Subject 99), "I try to make the best out of each situation" (Subject 60), and "For me each problem is solvable" (Subject 36). This motivational resource is often manifested in a clear-cut condemnation of suicide: Suicide is considered cowardly (whereas those who are more negativistic in their outlook on life tend to judge not committing but abstaining from committing as cowardly).

Generalized ego resources appeared already as structural implications of stage-specific suicide theories: In explaining suicidal acts, subjects made use of these dimensions. But over and beyond this more cognitive function, they also entered into subjects' attitudes toward suicide. Answers to the question "Do you think there can ever be a good reason for committing suicide?" showed that generalized ego resources—each individually—do protect from suicidal risks. Each one allows the individual to gain distance from the immediate pressure of the situation and to redefine the situation in such a way that a solution comes into sight. The following illustrate several of these dimensions:

Distancing via cyclical time conceptions
SUBJECT 84: (once considered suicide?): I wouldn't have done it because I thought, that'll pass, for I've had phases like that before.... From a distance, everything looks quite different, looks only half as bad.

Distancing via biographical time horizon
SUBJECT 89: Suicide is not right; just think if someone has a setback ... and right away kills himself ... after all, you've still got your whole life ahead of you.

Distancing via other life spheres
SUBJECT 97: Sometimes I think about suicide ... but then I weigh life and there are also beautiful aspects, in fact more than bad ones.

Expansion of the action space: consequences for others
SUBJECT 98: I've never understood, how one could kill oneself ... and that's what I always tell myself: I live for something, I'm needed, my parents do need me.

Self-reflexivity and self-objectivation as a means for self-regulation
SUBJECT 109: I've tried to redirect my thoughts by positive thinking. What really helps me is a good record. There are records of which I know that I really respond to them and to experience this swing: A minute ago I felt miserable and now I feel good again.

Rational goal setting, meaning of life as a task
SUBJECT 86 (describing a suicidal attempt): I was so depressed, everything was so negative.... Now I'm convinced that I'll be a dancer and I must dance, I must exist for my spectators and my parents.

SUBJECT 102 (had considered suicide): I've never really planned it, life should have a meaning somehow.

INTERVIEWER: What meaning?

SUBJECT 102: I think that's something you have to find out in life; it's like a key that you don't have from the beginning, but that you will find after a while, maybe.

These examples show that each of these general dimensions of ego development can function as a coping resource in dealing with suicidal impulses. While these dimensions, taken individually, help to open up alternatives to suicide in stressful situations, they are also integrated into the definition of suicide as an understandable and in this respect, to a certain extent, rational action. This is done in the commonsense suicide theories of different stages. These contribute to coping with suicide in a very specific way (over and beyond the general dimensions of ego development). Each stage-specific understanding of suicide implies a rejection of the suicidal motives of lower stages as inadequate and thus considerably narrows the range of legitimate reasons for committing suicide: Bad grades, trouble and conflicts in school, and so on no longer pass as justifiable motives.

That suicide theories function in this way is evidenced by the fact that several of our subjects who had attempted suicide disqualified their own former suicide attempts as "foolish." Thus, Subject 79 some time ago had attempted suicide because he had had difficulties finding a job and at the same time had had conflicts with his girlfriend. In our interview he commented on suicide as follows: "Most suicides are so desperate at the time, but in most cases things get better by themselves. People grow older and the situation somehow turns to the better. Yet, if, for example, a person is completely paralyzed after a traffic accident and for the rest of his life will be unable to move, in such a situation I can understand if he says, 'Okay, I put an end to myself.' But just because your girlfriend took off or you didn't get a job, those are no good reasons for throwing away one's life." This is not to deny, of course, that the remaining motives, because of their encompassing and motivationally deeply anchored structure, may prove to be all the more pressing and unescapable. Sociocognitive development does increase coping reasons, yet it may also increase risks.

Implications of a Cognitive Approach to Suicide

The reconstruction of commonsense suicide theories has theoretical as well as practical implications. In terms of theoretical implications, early suicide understanding corresponds to the trivial triggering theories on which newspaper headlines are based ("Bad Grades—Student Commits Suicide!"); thus, these are shown to be not altogether false. In the course of general ego development and specifically of development in suicide understanding, such triggering events come soon to be seen as utterly insufficient and illegitimate reasons for committing suicide. As has been shown, the experience of an intense adolescence crisis may advance suicide understanding and, by implication, coping resources for dealing with suicidal thoughts. This exemplifies what is commonly called growth through crisis resolution.

In terms of practical implications, the fact that quite a few adolescents in our sample seriously thought about suicide shows that suicidal impulses are to a certain degree a normal correlate of adolescence. At the same time, most of these subjects overcame this phase of being highly endangered and did so by normal sociocognitive growth. That is to say, adolescents at risk are in need of situational help for two reasons: They are confronted with special and unusual difficulties, and due to their limited ego resources they tend to be overwhelmed by situational pressures. In most cases, however, these are not indicators of pathological personality functioning but rather parts of normal development. Therefore, the help they need does not have to aim at changes in personality (for example, by therapy); an intervention into the temporary situation of the person may suffice. But the point must be stressed again: This practical implication holds for a sample of normal adolescents who come to terms with their problems without therapeutic help. It certainly does not hold for more serious cases of affective disorders.

References

Beckham, E. E. "Psychological Research in Depression and Suicide: A Historical Perspective." In C. F. Walker (ed.), *Clinical Psychology: Historical and Research Foundations. Applied Clinical Psychology*. New York: Plenum, 1991.

Bewskow, J. "Depression and Suicide." *Pharmacopsychiatry*, 1990, 23 (supplement 1), 3–8.

Borst, S., and Noam, G. G. "Suicidality and Psychopathology in Hospitalized Children and Adolescents." *Acta Paedopsychiatrica* 1989, 52, 165–175.

Döbert, R., and Nunner-Winkler, G. "Jugendliche schlagen über die Stränge. Abwehr-und Bewältigungsstrategien in moralisierbaren Handlungssituationen." In L. H. Eckensberger and R. K. Silbereisen (eds.), *Entwicklung sozialer Kognition: Paradigmen, Theorien, Ergebnisse*. Stuttgart, Germany: Klett-Cotta, 1980.

Döbert, R., and Nunner-Winkler, G. "Moralisches Urteilsniveau und Verlässlichkeit. Die Familie als Lernumwelt für kognitive und motivationale Aspekte des moralischen Bewusstseins in der Adoleszenz" [Moral development and personal reliability: The impact of the family on two aspects of moral consciousness in adolescence]. In G. Lind, A. H. Hartmann, and R. Wakenhut (eds.), *Moralisches Urteilen und soziale Umwelt*. Weinheim, Germany: Beltz, 1983.

Döbert, R., and Nunner-Winkler, G. "Interplay of Formal and Material Role-Taking in the Understanding of Suicide Among Adolescents and Young Adults. Part 1: Formal and Material Role-Taking." *Human Development*, 1985a, 28, 225–239.

Döbert, R., and Nunner-Winkler, G. "Interplay of Formal and Material Role-Taking in the Understanding of Suicide Among Adolescents and Young Adults. Part 2: Naive Suicide Theories and the Structural Approach." *Human Development*, 1985b, 28, 313–330.

Duggan, C. F., Sham, P., Lee, A. S., and Murray, R. M. "Can Future Suicidal Behavior in Depressed Patients Be Predicted?" *Journal of Affective Disorders*, 1991, 22 (3), 111–118.

Haan, N. "The Adolescent Antecedents of an Ego Model of Coping and Defense and Comparisons with Q-Sorted Ideal Personalities." *Genetic Psychology Monographs*, 1974, 89, 273–306.

Jacobs, D. *Suicide and Clinical Practice*. Washington, D.C.: American Psychiatry Press, 1992.

Katschnig, A., Sint, P., and Fuchs-Robetin, G. "Gibt es verschiedene Typen von Selbst-mordversuchen?" In W. Welz and H. Pohlheimer (eds.), *Selbstmordhandlungen. Suizid und Suizidversuch aus interdisziplinärer Sicht.* Weinheim, Germany: Beltz, 1981.

Marttunen, M. J., Aru, H., Henriksson, M. M., and Lönnqvist, J. K. "Mental Disorders in Adolescent Suicide: DSMIII-R Axes I and II Diagnoses in Suicides Among Thirteen- to Nineteen-Year-Olds in Finland." *Archives of General Psychiatry,* 1991, *48* (9), 834–839.

Pfeffer, C. R. "Attempted Suicide in Children and Adolescents: Causes and Management." In M. Lewis (ed.), *Child and Adolescent Psychiatry: A Comprehensive Textbook.* Baltimore: Williams and Wilkins, 1991.

Pfeffer, C. R. "Relationship Between Depression and Suicidal Behavior." In M. Shafii and S. L. Shafii (eds.), *Clinical Guide to Depression in Children and Adolescents.* Washington, D.C.: American Psychiatric Press, 1992.

Schmidtke, A., and Schaller, S. "Möglichkeiten und Grenzen testpsychologischer Diagnos-tik suizidalen Verhaltens." In R. Welz and H. Pohlheimer (eds.), *Selbstmordhandlungen. Suizid und Suizidversuch aus interdisziplinärer Sicht.* Weinheim, Germany: Beltz, 1981.

Selman, R. L., and Byrne, D. F. "A Structural-Developmental Analysis of Levels of Role-Taking in Middle Childhood." *Child Development,* 1974, *45,* 803–806.

RAINER DÖBERT is senior research sociologist at the Wissenschaftszentrum in Berlin, Germany.

GERTRUD NUNNER-WINKLER is senior scientist at the Max-Planck Institute for Psy-chological Research in Munich, Germany.

A clinical-developmental framework of adolescent suicidal behavior is presented, combining theory, research, and interview examples.

Developing Meaning, Losing Meaning: Understanding Suicidal Behavior in the Young

Gil G. Noam, Sophie Borst

Unsurpassed by any literary or scientific document about suicide, Goethe's (1774/1973) psychological portrait of Werther, more than two hundred years after its first publication, continues to generate deep insights into the wish to die in the young. No simple interpretation of this literary portrait suffices; it is as if we repeatedly look at a landscape while it changes right in front of our eyes. Similarly, our continued attempts to fully comprehend child and adolescent suicide elude even our best efforts.

In writing letters to his friend Wilhelm, the young man Werther not only discusses his growing love for Lotte and his increasing desperation but also presents an entire philosophy of life, a desire for unity in the development of self, and a careful description of the many meaningless conventions of adulthood. Werther's preoccupations are with Lotte, but their tragic relationship becomes the container for an even deeper despair about Werther's unwillingness to accept the world as he finds it.

Psychological interpretations of Werther have sprung up over the centuries: The triangle among Lotte, Werther, and Albert (Lotte's husband) has inspired psychoanalysts, for example, to an oedipal understanding. Werther's diminishing ability to develop alternative modes of thought and feeling, coupled with a despair that far outweighs his relational troubles, has led others to suspect an affective disorder, or even a psychotic depression. But we have

---

We thank William Calder for his many excellent comments and editorial changes, which have strengthened this chapter considerably.

learned too little by making such statements, for these interpretations describe only the most relevant dimensions while making them primary explanations. In Werther, as in most cases, suicidal behavior is related to a complex set of meanings and experiences, a final pathway of an intricate variety of problems. In an important passage of the story, Werther makes this point himself: " 'Why must people like you,' I exclaimed, 'when you discuss any action, immediately say: "This is foolish, that is wise; this is good, that is bad!" And what does it all mean? Does it mean that you have really discovered the inner circumstances of an action? Do you know how to explain definitely the reason why it happened, why it had to happen? If you indeed knew, you would be less hasty in your judgments' " (Goethe, 1973, p. 57).

Indeed, we must surpass the desire to simplify, to moralize or pathologize in order to gain access to the many facets and factors that bring about the wish to die. The clinical-developmental perspective on adolescent suicidal behavior, an approach we take in this chapter, pursues such a goal through theory, quantitative studies with psychiatrically hospitalized adolescents, and qualitative clinical data. This perspective posits a lifelong changing pattern of meanings about self and relationships as well as developing interaction patterns with significant others. Much evidence has been forthcoming that suicidal children and adolescents are often partaking in destructive family, peer, and romantic relationships (for example, Asarnow, Carlson, and Guthrie, 1987; Campbell, Milling, Laughlin, and Bush, 1993; Blumenthal, 1990). Furthermore, suicidal adolescents, like their nonsuicidal peers, are actively engaged in cognitively organizing meanings about themselves, their relationships, and their lives (for example, Noam, Powers, Kilkenny, and Beedy, 1990). These meanings contribute to what the adolescent interprets as especially destructive, pain producing, and suicide generating.

Suicidal Behavior and Social-Cognitive Development: The Clinical-Developmental Perspective

Epidemiological studies consistently find that attempted suicide, while relatively rare in childhood, becomes a serious threat in the adolescent years. Incidents of suicide attempts show a sharp rise at ages thirteen to fourteen (Carlson and Cantwell, 1982; Rutter and Garmezy, 1983). According to a review of ten community survey studies of high school students, 2.4 percent to 20 percent of the students attempted suicide in the previous year (Diekstra, 1993). Within at-risk populations, such as hospitalized psychiatric patients, suicidal preoccupations and behavior are often the main reason for hospitalization.

The question of what might contribute to the great increase of suicidal behavior in the adolescent years has puzzled many clinicians and researchers. Interesting patterns have begun to emerge from the application of principles from development and psychopathology. For example, some investigators have suggested that early pubertal onset increases the risk of suicide because it contributes to a biopsychosocial imbalance (Diekstra, 1993). Others have speculated that formal operational levels of cognitive development are a necessary but not sufficient condition for experiencing despair, self-hate, and hopelessness, all contributing to suicidal ideation and suicidal behavior (Carlson, Asarnow, and Orbach, 1987; Shaffer and Fisher, 1981). Similarly, Rutter (1986) hypothesized that the rise in depression and suicidality in adolescents might be due to cognitive advances such as self-observation and future orientation. Noam and others (in press) found that social-cognitive development is related to increased levels of depression in adolescent psychiatric patients when compared to a delayed group of age-matched peers. These findings can be usefully interpreted in the tradition of Piaget, Werner, Vygotsky, and others, all of whom have contributed to the establishment of the clinical-developmental point of view. This perspective follows a number of assumptions introduced in earlier publications (for example, Noam, 1988; Noam and Valiant, 1994). We briefly mention three assumptions relevant to our research on suicide.

Development of Meaning. For clinical-developmental psychologists, the transformation of mental representations of self and relationships has been a base on which to build a perspective of psychopathology. Many cross-sectional and longitudinal studies have shown that children, adolescents, and even adults shape and reshape their understanding of the social world. Piaget's (1932) early work on the moral judgment of the child was a milestone in the research on developmental differences in how children construct and perceive social rules. Since then, many developmental perspectives of the social world have been introduced, including the domains of social perspective taking, moral development, conceptions of conventions, and the self. All of these studies about different domains of social development share the idea that developmental levels are best understood in terms of the complexity of the representation of social reality. They also share, even after most researchers have given up the idea of a simple stagewise progression of cognitive function, the notion that these representations develop in some logical form from less mature and differentiated to more complex and integrated.

While the initial work has been mostly on tracing the normative pathways in development, a great many implications are emerging for the study of dysfunctional pathways. Because we assume that identical events can be experienced differently depending on the developmental level of cognition, social cognition, and socioemotional development, clinical-developmental psychologists focus not only on behaviors and symptoms but also and simultaneously on the meanings that these problem behaviors hold for the individual. For example, attempted suicide can be part of a carefully planned and cognitively complex set of operations, or an impulsive decision, without consideration for the consequences of the behavior. At present, little is known about how the complexity of thought relates to the understanding, maintenance, and evolution of symptoms and syndromes. Uncovering connections between the better-explored world of social cognition and mental representations and the relatively unknown area of their relationship to dysfunctions makes clinical-developmental psychology an exciting new area of inquiry.

Age Chronology. From these assumptions about development come significant questions about the usefulness of chronological age in the study of development and psychopathology. Today, we know about interesting age trends in psychopathology. For example, certain phobias and anxieties, such as separation anxiety and nightmares, are especially prevalent in early childhood and tend to decrease in middle childhood. Suicide rates rise dramatically in adolescence, and so do a number of other disorders, such as obsessive-compulsive behavior, depression, and conduct problems. Age can serve as a simple organizer of many underlying processes. But the simplicity of an age approach is deceptive. When we study mental representations and meaning systems, we quickly find that age is by no means a guarantor that basic cognitive and social-cognitive processes have actually occurred. Many adolescents and adults, for example, do not ever reach formal operational thought, even though most charts used in textbooks juxtapose this developmental level with adolescence. These charts reflect, of course, a common misapplication of the theory. That many adolescents function at the formal operational level is empirically true. But the fact remains that adolescence does not necessarily precipitate a transformation in cognitive development. Some adolescents continue to function at concrete operational levels and use these capacities for the rest of their lives. If we use chronological age as our developmental psychopathology marker, we miss the fact that many of our subjects and patients within one age group use fundamentally different tools to construct their internal and interpersonal realities (Noam, 1988; Noam, Recklitis, and Paget, 1991). For that reason, we study the complexity of meaning systems along cognitive, social, and emotional lines and in relation to symptoms, syndromes, or types of maladaptations.

Development and Dysfunction. Clinical-developmental psychology is not simply an application of cognitive psychology to the realm of psychological dysfunction. Instead, it reformulates many traditionally held assumptions of normative theory. For example, the idea that higher stages of development are more adaptive, as claimed by Piaget and Kohlberg, requires serious reconsideration from a developmental psychopathology perspective. The same capacity that can produce more self-knowledge and adaptation can also be used for more complex forms of self-deception and self-destruction, such as suicidal behavior (Noam, 1993).

Ego Development and Suicidality: A Line of Research

With these principles in mind, we embarked on a systematic study of suicidal behavior to assess whether our theoretical assumptions and clinical observations pertaining to a developmental typology of suicidality would hold up under more rigorous empirical scrutiny. We decided that Loevinger's (1976) concept of ego development would be a most useful tool for suicide research because of its developmental focus on impulse control, experience of guilt, and complexity of emotional experience. The ego, as defined by Loevinger, is the master trait around which personality is constructed. The assumption is that each person has a frame of reference that systematically organizes his or her experience of self and other people. There are nine stages along which these frames of reference may be grouped. However, for our research, we focused on the important distinction between what Loevinger calls preconformist (Stages 2, Delta, and Delta/3) and conformist (Stages 3 and 3/4) developmental levels. Preconformist adolescents have a concrete, egocentric perspective on self and others. They tend to be impulsive and to have exploitative relationships. With increased development, an adolescent becomes capable of taking another person's perspective and achieves the capacity for empathy. Conformist adolescents are therefore more likely to be concerned about being liked and accepted and often express their views in clichés and stereotypes. They often see themselves through the eyes of other people and show more cognitive complexity than do preconformist adolescents.

We hypothesized that, in a clinical sample, the more mature, conformist developmental positions would show a higher incidence of suicidal behavior and ideation. But we wanted to study the developmental dimensions always in the context of other risk factors—in this case, age, gender, and psychiatric disorders. Our subjects were 219 early adolescent patients between the ages of twelve and sixteen who had a DSM-III diagnosis (as measured by the Diagnostic Interview Schedule for Children [DISC]; see Costello and others, 1984) of affective disorder, conduct disorder, or both. Ego development was measured by using the Washington University Sentence Completion Test (Loevinger, Wessler, and Redmore, 1970).

As predicted, we found that girls were more likely to attempt suicide than boys; one-half of the girls had attempted suicide, compared to only one-fifth of the boys. Attempters were more likely to be diagnosed with affective or mixed conduct-affective disorders rather than conduct disorders. Of the conduct-disordered adolescents, only 12 percent had attempted suicide, compared to 51 percent of the adolescents with an affective disorder and 55 percent of the adolescents with a mixed conduct-affective disorder. Furthermore, we demonstrated a significant relation between suicide attempts and developmental complexity, with the conformist adolescents being more likely to attempt suicide than the preconformist adolescents. Of the conformist adolescents, 62 percent were suicidal, compared to only 32 percent of the preconformist adolescents. This correlation continued to be significant when gender and diagnosis were controlled for. By means of stepwise logistic regression, we found that a model including gender, diagnosis, and ego development could predict the suicidal status of 76 percent of the sample correctly. This study further supported the importance of transcending age as the key developmental variable, as we did not find any association between age and suicide attempts in this adolescent sample. Instead, the adolescents' frame of reference proved to be a useful concept for understanding developmental dimensions of suicidality.

In line with the ego developmental construct, we have given our findings the following possible interpretation: With the social-cognitive reorganization that normally occurs in adolescence, the unhappiness that could formerly be attributed to external sources and dealt with behaviorally becomes increasingly part of inner evaluations of the self. Such transformation is likely to lead to more self-blame and overtly self-destructive symptomatology as typical reactions to interpersonal disappointments (for example, Noam, 1988).

Our findings also support the concept that more mature ego stages can be associated with maladaptive and personally injurious behaviors. In fact, paradoxically, our study suggests that a delay in development can function as a protective factor for suicidal behavior rather than serve necessarily as a suicide risk factor. The self-protective and externalizing qualities of the earlier developmental positions put a person at greater risk for impulsivity, acting-out problems, and delinquency. Yet, they may shield the adolescent from directing the aggression against the self, since the problem is mainly viewed as externally located.

These findings further suggest that there is not one suicidal type. For example, on a diagnostic level we found suicidal adolescents who were depressed, conduct-disordered, or with both a depression and a conduct disorder. Using the ego development model, we found a group of suicidal adolescents who were delayed in their development, necessitating a systematic study about different types we had posited conceptually before (Noam, 1987). We became convinced that the subtyping would be of great practical importance because most advances for clinical interventions depend on a deepened understanding of the different processes involved in seemingly identical actions, such as suicidal behavior.

The idea of subtyping suicidal adolescents is, of course, not new, and two main subtypes of suicide attempters have been defined: those who are primarily impulsive and aggressive, and those who are primarily depressed and show little, if any, aggressive behavior (Brent and others, 1988; Pfeffer and others, 1989). Brent and others (1988) demonstrated that the aggressive type makes impulsive attempts of variable intent, while the depressive type is hopeless and makes planned attempts of high suicide intent. Similarly, Shaffer (1974) delineated three types of child and adolescent suicide completers: depressed, delinquent, and mixed depressed and delinquent. Pfeffer and others (1989) found important differences between adolescents who were both assaultive and suicidal and adolescents who were only suicidal. Thus far, these subtypes have been predominantly classified on the basis of symptomatology. As mentioned earlier, developmental psychopathology research has suggested that an adolescent's developmental level might be an important moderator of symptom expression (see Kazdin, 1989). Thus, we became convinced that social-cognitive development plays an important role in understanding the differences among the various suicidal profiles that have been delineated.

Specifically, we predicted that the adolescent attempters functioning at a preconformist level of ego development present as overtly angry, impulsive, and concrete and have great difficulty taking the perspectives of other people. On the other hand, attempters functioning at conformist developmental levels were expected to be more self-blaming and depressed. For that reason, we labeled the first group "angry-defiant" and the second group "self-blaming." In order to test these hypotheses, we conducted a study (Borst and Noam, 1993) for which we selected fifty-two females, ages thirteen to sixteen, admitted to a locked inpatient psychiatric unit. These girls were each reported to have made a serious suicidal attempt within six months of admission. Based on Loevinger's measure of ego development (Sentence Completion Test), the girls were divided into two groups: preconformist ($N = 29$) and conformist ($N = 23$) developmental levels. Both groups were similar in age and socioeconomic status. Girls were selected for multiple reasons. First, they are more likely to attempt suicide than boys. Second, gender is associated with other variables of interest in our study: Girls are more often diagnosed with affective disorders (Noam and others, in press; Rutter and Garmezy, 1983) and tend to function at higher levels of ego development during adolescence compared to boys (Noam and others, in press; Hauser, Jacobson, Noam, and Powers, 1983; Redmore and Loevinger, 1979).

The first issue of interest in our study was the role of internalizing and externalizing symptoms in both developmental types. We used the Achenbach and Edelbrock Youth Self-Report symptom checklist (YSR), and DISC, mentioned before, which generates DSM-III diagnoses. Based on the YSR data, we found that the preconformist and the conformist attempters were similar on internalizing symptomatology. However, as predicted, the preconformist attempters reported significantly more externalizing symptomatology. On a diagnostic level, similar results were found: The majority of suicidal girls, 86 percent in both groups, were diagnosed with an affective disorder. Again, the conformist girls were significantly more often diagnosed with pure affective disorders (48 percent versus 10 percent), while the preconformist girls were significantly more often diagnosed with mixed conduct affective disorders (76 percent versus 39 percent).

Defenses were measured using the adolescent version of the Defense Mechanisms Inventory, a paper-and-pencil test measuring five defense clusters. Significant differences in defense styles were found between the two developmental groups. The preconformist attempters used significantly more externalizing defenses, or turning-against-other, which includes defenses of displacement, regression, and identification with the aggressor. The conformist attempters used more internalizing defenses, such as reversal, which includes denial and reaction formation, and principalization, which involves the defenses of intellectualization, rationalization, and isolation of affect. Both groups scored similarly on the defense cluster of turning-against-self. This finding was not surprising since this defense cluster has been found to strongly discriminate between suicidal and nonsuicidal patients in general, in both adult and adolescent samples (Scholz, 1973; Recklitis, Noam, and Borst, 1992).

The results support the notion that there are two developmental types of female suicide attempters, who differ significantly in symptomatology, diagnosis, and defensive style. Preconformist attempters, the angry-defiant type, presented as suicidal with both depression and aggression as well as externalizing defense mechanisms. Conformist attempters, the self-blaming type, presented with depression and used more internalizing defenses to cope with conflict. They tended to spend less time in physical restraints than the preconformist girls. The conformist girls were restrained for self-destructive behavior rather than assaultive behavior, and the restraining was generally limited to one incident. The preconformist attempters, on the other hand, were more often restrained for assaultive behavior. We concluded that developmental dimensions appear to play an important role in understanding differences among suicidal girls.

Qualitative Analyses of the Developmental Typology

As a next step, we started a more in-depth empirical exploration of qualitative data, for which we developed a semistructured clinical-developmental suicide interview that inquires about the experience and construction of the suicidal event. In addition, we developed a manual to code the interview material. To date, a subsample of females from our empirical study described above has been interviewed (Jonckheer, 1992). Two brief vignettes are presented here to illustrate this qualitative study and our empirical data on developmental typologies of suicidal females. These two respondents, an angry-defiant suicidal girl, functioning at the preconformist developmental level, and a self-blaming suicidal girl, functioning at the conformist developmental level, were interviewed about their suicide attempts and their views on the events that led up to the suicidal behavior. Instead of focusing on the commonalities of these and other suicidal females, we highlight here distinctions in the way the suicidal crisis is understood and experienced.

Vignette 1: Yolanda. Yolanda is a typical example of the angry-defiant suicidal type. She was a fifteen-year-old, white, overweight, and the oldest of three children. She was transferred to our center from an emergency room, where she was taken by her mother after she told her mother that she would be dead by the next morning. Two weeks before, she had cut her wrists, but not seriously enough to require medical intervention. She also described having overdosed on pills, not specifying the date and type of drugs. This was her first psychiatric hospitalization, although she had received some counseling at age nine because of depression and feelings of low self-esteem. Her parents were divorced about one year before her hospitalization. During the interview, she talked of despising her father for having treated her badly. On one occasion, she had slashed his car tires with a knife.

Given this history, it was understandable why she was so self-protective in her relationships. For example, she stated, "I don't like to get close to people because I feel I can't trust anybody." She felt that way with "everybody in my life" and thought that her father contributed significantly to her mistrust. It became clear that Yolanda was very lonely, without a single person she could confide in. She also experienced little support from and intimacy with her mother, a fact she puzzled over at times: "My mother is not all the way behind me but I don't know why."

Yolanda spoke of her suicidality in rather concrete ways, focusing on discrete events in the "here and now." She pointed to a fight with her mother over coming home late as the reason for her most recent attempt. After her mother yelled at her and made her eat alone in another room, Yolanda took a razor and cut herself. When asked why this fight made her suicidal, she stated, "Because it was three (mother and siblings) to one." Yolanda felt that her mother could do a better job of parenting, but this was not something she ever talked about with her mother. As is quite typical for the angry-defiant adolescent, we found a strong emphasis on dealing independently with life: "I can stand alone; I've done it for the past fifteen years," and "Nobody has ever supported me that I can remember, ever." Another motive for the suicide attempt, Yolanda said, was "to get frustration out." Yolanda felt badly that her last suicide attempt was unsuccessful. If she had died, she thought, she would have gone to heaven and her mother would have felt "bad, but on the other hand, it's like a big relief off her shoulder because she wouldn't have to deal with the fights, the arguments." This element of revenge is an important motive in many angry-defiant adolescents.

In keeping with our earlier empirical findings, Yolanda described feeling both sad and angry. She felt depressed about being ugly and a failure. She felt angry about "everything, the world." She saw herself as a "tough kid" and also described her girlfriends as tough, with "problems worse than mine." These friends seemed to offer very little emotional support and they did not talk about problems or feelings. They also got into serious fistfights with other groups of girls. A close friend, Yolanda said, is someone who defends her if she is attacked.

During the interview, she still felt acutely suicidal. She did not experience the hospital treatment as helpful but rather as a punishment designed to give her mother "a break." She could not think of anything that would make her feel better; the only thing she wanted for the future was "to die."

Vignette 2: Anna. Anna is an example of the self-blaming suicidal type, functioning at the more complex, conformist developmental level. She was an attractive fifteen-year-old, who was living with her mother, stepfather, and younger stepsister. This was her second psychiatric hospitalization, and she was admitted because she felt acutely suicidal and depressed and had been cutting herself for a number of months.

Anna described suffering from periods of hopelessness, helplessness, and feeling lonely with decreased energy. Anna's parents divorced when she was four years old after a long period of parental discord. She felt that her parents' divorce had a big impact on her: "I guess when I was twelve, it was the first time when I started thinking about suicide. I was really upset a lot of times, I might have had a lot of anger left over from my parents' divorce that I never really shared and now I can't really remember what it was about.... I did vent it somewhat on my dad though, since I used to get aggravated with him a lot and I would just start hitting him and stuff.... But after a while I realized that it wasn't right."

Anna felt that life was not worth living after she had a fight with her father: "It was right after my dad had just sworn at me and called me all these names. He had never done that before. He always had been really gentle with me and so that really scared me a lot. I guess that brushed me off the edge. It made me feel really alone. Like nobody would care so why don't I just die." Anna seemed to blame herself for this fight and the resulting suicidal crisis: "I don't know, but I didn't want him to think it was his fault because it wasn't. I mean I am sure it had something to do that I deserved it or I did provoke him to call me these names. It was also me not being able to deal with it at the time that pushed me there. It wasn't his fault, he lost his temper and that's only human." She described the attempt as follows: "I was just like 'Oh well, my dad doesn't love me anymore, no one cares about me, my mom is always yelling at me,' and stuff like that. It wasn't a rational thought at that time, like impulsive almost."

When Anna described difficulties relating to her mother, she showed remarkable sensitivity to her mother's problems and seemed to protect her mother from her own criticism: "My mom is trying really hard to work things out, but I have this feeling that she can't understand because there have been so many misunderstandings in the past that when it comes to this stuff I don't want to tell her because she probably doesn't understand it or is taking it the wrong way or is taking it personally as a defense towards herself. I also don't want her to worry too much so I don't tell her much." Both of her parents were struggling with their own problems, and just before Anna's hospitalization her father needed to be hospitalized as well for depression and suicidal plans.

Even though Anna acknowledged feeling angry, this was rarely directed against her environment, as she poignantly illustrated with the following statement: "I just kind of shut it all inside and this doesn't work. I can't shove my anger inside and hope it will go away because it doesn't. So it kind of turns into sadness because I don't like being angry so I get sad instead."

Anna also found it difficult to share her problems with her peers because she was afraid this would hurt them, or that they would not accept her anymore. She described telling her best friend of her suicidal preoccupations and how it ruined the relationship: "The major issues in my life right now are around my depression and that can be really scary for people to hear, especially my friends. This is why I can't really share the major issues of my life with anyone."

At the time of the interview, Anna had become less suicidal, but her reason for living was found outside herself: "I guess right now I don't think I would commit suicide. Because enough people have told me it would really devastate them that I couldn't go through with it, just for my own relief. It is too selfish, I really don't want to hurt anyone."

Interpretation. What these two suicidal girls, and the other girls we interviewed, had in common was their despair and loneliness. They all believed that there was no one to turn to. All of them experienced a breakdown of relationships with parents or peers, or both, as one of the precipitating events leading up to the suicidal crisis. In the literature, there is considerable convergence of findings about the role of decrease in self-esteem and interpersonal problems between the adolescent and his or her parents (Blumenthal, 1990; Gilligan, Lyons, and Hanner, 1990). A number of studies have demonstrated that suicidal children and adolescents perceive their families as more conflictual and less cohesive (Asarnow, Carlson, and Guthrie, 1987; Campbell, Milling, Laughlin, and Bush, 1993) and have less active and communicative relationships with their fathers (King and others, 1990). Family cohesion has also been found to be a protective factor against suicidal behavior (Rubenstein and others, 1989).

Yolanda and Anna were overwhelmed by their painful affects at the time of their suicide attempts. However, they seemed to understand these experiences in radically different ways. As our empirical studies have suggested, and these two vignettes support, differences in personality development contribute to different clinical presentations. Anna, like the majority of self-blaming suicidal females, was much more "psychologically minded," whereas Yolanda, like the majority of angry-defiant suicidal females, seemed to lack a certain psychological insight. In addition to different ways of understanding and expressing themselves, the two girls had different symptoms and ways of coping. Yolanda presented with a combination of depression and aggression and frequently got into physical fights with her parents and peers. Anna was more manifestly anxious and depressed, and both her self-blaming behavior and fear of being selfish were in the foreground. She seemed to have "swallowed" all of her anger. Yolanda told us that she did not trust anybody and found no comfort in talking with others, whereas Anna described relationships with others as a valuable means of getting help. This trust issue also became apparent during the interview where Yolanda, like most angry-defiant girls, stayed very much on guard and remained mostly nonrevealing. In contrast, Anna seemed motivated to talk about her problems.

As Yolanda showed, angry-defiant suicidal females have limited perspective on knowing why relationships with significant others are experienced as problematic. Girls like Yolanda feel that their families are not taking care of them and that they are not understood, which makes them very angry at their environments. It is important not to attribute Yolanda's interpretations to internal constructions but to interpersonal experiences that have validity. But it is also important to note that in the universe of complex interactions between her and her mother, Yolanda's developmental frame of meaning pulled espe-cially for the negative, rejecting and punitive without much understanding of the dilemmas that confronted her parents. While there are, of course, family environments that are "all bad," Yolanda's family environment had a number of positive attributes that could not come to the fore due to the destructive interaction patterns.

Angry-defiant suicidal adolescents often express the strong feeling that they have no control over their lives. They feel punished without good reasons, entrapped and powerless. They view their suicidality as a concrete form of boundary setting, as a way to "get out." A number of angry-defiant girls in our study mentioned revenge on their parent as the main motive for their suicide attempts: "Maybe when I die my family will realize that they had a daughter who died because they didn't treat the kid the way they were supposed to."

Self-blaming suicidal adolescents typically have a broader perspective. Anna, for example, was able to indicate a range of precipitating events, often interpersonal disappointments, that contributed to her feeling suicidal. She framed events historically and was able to verbalize a notion of change. She explained her motivation for her own behavior and also was able to put her-self in her parents' position. This strength turned into a weakness, however, as she blamed herself for not having a good relationship with her parents. Like Anna, most self-blaming adolescents have difficulty expressing criticism. It is crucial for them to be liked and appreciated in order to feel a sense of self-worth. They do not like to be overtly angry because it threatens relationships, which triggers strong separation anxieties. Others' angry behavior is consid-ered "only human," while their own anger makes them feel very bad. Contrary to the angry-defiant girls, they engage in more intimate relationships but then often seem to experience a loss of sense of self. They become extremely vul-nerable, particularly when the significant people in their lives are critical or blaming. Guilt often plays a powerful role in their suicides.

We also noticed developmental differences in the nature of the suicide attempts. The angry-defiant adolescents often made impulsive attempts that were action-oriented. For example, we interviewed a girl who, after an argu-ment with her mother, became so angry and upset that she jumped out of a window. It became clear during the interview that she had not thought at all about the possible lethal consequences of her action. The self-blaming adoles-cents, on the contrary, often had thought about suicide for some time and tended to take drug overdoses. They were more likely to have written moving good-bye notes mentioning that they did not want to be burdens anymore.

Gaining Further Perspective on Suicidal Youth

Our work has further convinced us of the complexity of multiple risk factors in suicidal adolescents. Suicide signifies in most adolescents a serious break-down of meaning, a loss of hope and faith in the future. We are convinced that without access to the internal and interpersonal meanings, we remain outside the phenomenon that suicide represents to us all: adolescent, clinician, teacher, and researcher.

Our work focuses mostly on children and adolescents from toxic family and peer environments, who often look back on abusive pasts and who understandably have lost a sense of positive meaning about their futures. For them, there is usually a great deal of hope if they are placed in supportive environments, or if the existing families receive the massive interventions they often need. Suicidal children and adolescents need productive relationships with peers and adults to help them gain new confidence and provide them with a sense of control beyond the ability to end their lives. And they often need psychiatric and psychological intervention to help them with impulsivity, delinquency, depression, and anxiety. Their longstanding problems have often been internalized and have created an inner milieu of self-aggression that requires knowledgeable and differentiated forms of intervention.

It is often not only the patient and the family who are not cooperating in the attempt to establish good interventions; in many cases our knowledge base remains too rudimentary to produce the needed maps for intervention. To this day, in building our frameworks we have tried too hard to establish descriptions of *the* suicidal child and adolescent, instead of entering the meaning world of each child and adolescent far enough to get a hold of the organizing cognitive, emotional, and behavioral factors responsible for suicide. Because such meanings are so different in each child, clinicians usually like to pursue specifics in each case, and researchers are more interested in group rather than individual differences. But when we look at these children from a clinical-developmental perspective, we can, in fact, make some generalizations. One way of doing so is to organize typical meanings, including those related to suicide, around a developmental continuum. This has been our strategy, and our studies on ego development and suicidal behavior suggest that social-cognitive development plays an important role in the emergence and expression of suicidal behavior in young adolescents.

Adequate knowledge about the developmental worlds of suicidal children and adolescents entails more than what we have done to date. We have chosen the broad developmental distinctions of an overall frame of meaning, one that Loevinger calls ego development. Needed now are ways to relate these broad attempts at structuring cohesive experience with subdomains of development (for example, Damon, 1977; Noam, 1993). These include ways of reflecting on one's biography, skills in role taking, impulse control, evolution of hopefulness and hopelessness, and so on. The possibilities seem endless, and the closer the developmental phenomena relate to those processes implied in suicide, the more scientific advances we can expect.

An understanding of the developmental components in suicidal children and adolescents is critical because it enables us to better guide our interventions. For us, our research has resulted in better clinical interventions not simply as a set of simple techniques but foremost as a grid for guiding a process of exploration. We are still confronted with an unanswered question, as in the case of Werther with whom we began this chapter. What would it have taken to save his young life, without ignoring the fundamental questions he asked of life and love? Could he have been saved if someone had been able to enter his world, his preoccupations, his emotional fluctuations? If we develop better maps of the internal and interpersonal worlds of hopelessness and create a more complex and encompassing language to differentiate experiences that on the surface look identical, can we then engender hope and a renewed faith in life? Because where isolation and despair rule, a human contact is created. Being understood cannot take the place of containment and help in controlling impulses, but it creates a starting point in a process that can make the difference between life and death.

References

Asarnow, J., Carlson, G., and Guthrie, D. "Coping Strategies, Self-Perceptions, Hopelessness, and Perceived Family Environments in Depressed and Suicidal Children." *Journal of Consulting and Clinical Psychology,* 1987, 55, 361–366.

Blumenthal, S. "An Overview and Synopsis of Risk Factors, Assessment, and Treatment of Suicidal Patients Over the Life Cycle." In S. Blumenthal and D. J. Kupfer (eds.), *Suicide Over the Life Cycle: Risk Factors, Assessment, and Treatment.* Washington, D.C.: American Psychiatric Press, 1990.

Borst, S., and Noam, G. G. "Developmental Psychopathology in Suicidal and Non-Suicidal Adolescent Girls." *Journal of the American Academy of Child and Adolescent Psychiatry,* 1993, 32, 501–508.

Brent, D., Perper, J., Goldstein, C., Kolko, D., Allan, M., Allman, C., and Zelenak, J. "Risk Factors for Adolescent Suicide: A Comparison of Adolescent Suicide Victims with Suicidal Inpatients." *Archives of General Psychiatry,* 1988, 45, 581–588.

Campbell, N., Milling, L., Laughlin, A., and Bush, E. "The Psychosocial Climate of Families with Suicidal Pre-Adolescent Children." *American Journal of Orthopsychiatry,* 1993, 63, 142–145.

Carlson, G. A., Asarnow, J. R., and Orbach, I. "Developmental Aspects of Suicidal Behavior in Children, Part 1." *Journal of the American Academy of Child and Adolescent Psychiatry,* 1987, 26, 186–192.

Carlson, G. A., and Cantwell, D. P. "Suicidal Behavior and Depression in Children and Adolescents." *Journal of the American Academy of Child and Adolescent Psychiatry,* 1982, 21, 361–368.

Costello, A., Edelbrock, C., Dulcan, M., Kalas, R., and Klaric, S. *Development and Testing of the NIMH Diagnostic Interview Schedule for Children in a Clinical Population: Final Report.* Contract RFP-DB-81-0027. Rockville, Md.: Center for Epidemiologic Studies, National Institute for Mental Health, 1984.

Damon, W. *The Social World of the Child.* San Francisco: Jossey-Bass, 1977.

Diekstra, R. "Depression and Suicidal Behavior in Adolescence." In M. Rutter (ed.), *Psychosocial Problems of Youth.* New York: Cambridge University Press, 1993.

Gilligan, C., Lyons, N., and Hanner, T. (eds.). *Making Connections: The Relational World of Adolescent Girls at the Emma Willard School.* Cambridge, Mass.: Harvard University Press, 1990.

Goethe, J. W. *The Sorrows of Young Werther.* (E. Mayer and L. Bogan, trans.) New York: Vintage Books, 1973. (Originally published 1774.)

Hauser, S., Jacobson, A., Noam, G., and Powers, S. "Ego Development and Self-Image Complexity in Early Adolescence: Longitudinal Studies of Diabetic and Psychiatric Patients." *Archives of General Psychiatry*, 1983, *40*, 325–332.

Jonckheer, J. "Developmental Dimensions of Suicidality." Unpublished master's thesis, Vakgroep Klinische Psychologie, Universiteit van Amsterdam, 1992.

Kazdin, A. E. "Developmental Psychopathology." *American Psychologist*, 1989, *44*, 180–187.

King, C. A., Raskin, A., Gdowski, C. L., Butkus, M., and Opipari, L. "Psychosocial Factors Associated with Urban Adolescent Female Suicide Attempts." *Journal of the American Academy of Child and Adolescent Psychiatry*, 1990, *29*, 289–294.

Loevinger, J. *Ego Development: Conceptions and Theories.* San Francisco: Jossey-Bass, 1976.

Loevinger, J., Wessler, R., and Redmore, C. *Measuring Ego Development.* Vol. 2: *Scoring Manual for Women and Girls.* San Francisco: Jossey-Bass, 1970.

Noam, G. "Clinical-Developmental Psychology: Implications for Understanding Child and Adolescent Suicide." Paper presented at Children and Adolescents in Jeopardy: A Clinical-Developmental Perspective of Suicidal Youth conference at McLean Hospital/Harvard University Medical School, Belmont, Mass., Apr. 1987.

Noam, G. G. "A Constructivist Approach to Developmental Psychopathology." In E. D. Nannis and P. A. Cowan (eds.), *Developmental Psychopathology and Its Treatment.* New Directions for Child Development, no. 39. San Francisco: Jossey-Bass, 1988.

Noam, G. G. "Development as the Aim of Clinical Intervention." *Development and Psychopathology*, 1992, *4*, 679–696.

Noam, G. G. "Ego Development: True or False?" *Psychological Inquiry*, 1993, *4*, 43–48.

Noam, G. G., Paget, K., Valiant, G., Borst, S., and Bartok, J. "Conduct and Affective Disorders in Developmental Perspective: A Systematic Study of Adolescent Developmental Psychopathology." *Development and Psychopathology*, in press.

Noam, G. G., Powers, S., Kilkenny, R., and Beedy, J. "The Interpersonal Self in Life-Span Developmental Perspective: Theory, Measurement, and Longitudinal Case Studies." In P. B. Baltes, D. L. Featherman, and R. M. Lerner (eds.), *Life-Span Development and Behavior.* Vol. 10. Hillsdale, N.J.: Erlbaum, 1990.

Noam, G. G., Recklitis, C., and Paget, K. "Pathways of Ego Development: Contributions to Maladaptation and Adjustment." *Development and Psychopathology*, 1991, *3*, 311–321.

Noam, G. G., and Valiant, G. "Clinical-Developmental Psychology in Developmental Psychopathology: Theory and Research of an Emerging Perspective." In D. Cicchetti and S. Toth (eds.), *Disorders and Dysfunctions of the Self.* Rochester Symposia on Developmental Psychopathology. Vol. 5. Rochester, N.Y.: University of Rochester Press, 1994.

Pfeffer, C. R., Newcorn, J., Kaplan, G., Mizruchi, M. S., and Plutchik, R. "Subtypes of Suicidal and Assaultive Behaviors in Adolescent Psychiatric Patients: A Research Note." *Journal of Child Psychology and Psychiatry and Allied Disciplines*, 1989, *30*, 151–163.

Piaget, J. *The Moral Judgment of the Child.* Orlando, Fla.: Harcourt Brace Jovanovich, 1932.

Recklitis, C., Noam, G. G., and Borst, S. "Adolescent Suicide and Defensive Style." *Suicide and Life-Threatening Behavior*, 1992, *22*, 374–387.

Redmore, C., and Loevinger, J. "Ego Development in Adolescence: Longitudinal Studies." *Journal of Youth and Adolescence*, 1979, *8*, 1–20.

Rubenstein, J., Heeren, T., Housman, D., Rubin, C., and Stechler, G. "Suicidal Behavior in 'Normal' Adolescents: Risk and Protective Factors." *American Journal of Orthopsychiatry*, 1989, *59*, 59–71.

Rutter, M. "The Developmental Psychopathology of Depression: Issues and Perspectives." In M. Rutter, C. E. Izard, and P. B. Read (eds.), *Depression in Young People: Developmental and Clinical Perspectives.* New York: Guilford, 1986.

Rutter, M., and Garmezy, N. "Developmental Psychopathology." In E. M. Hetherington (ed.), *Handbook of Child Psychology.* Vol. 4: *Socialization, Personality, and Social Development.* New York: Wiley, 1983.

Scholz, J. A. "Defense Styles in Suicide Attempters." *Journal of Consulting and Clinical Psychology*, 1973, *41* 70–73.
Shaffer, D. "Suicide in Childhood and Early Adolescence." *Journal of Child Psychology and Psychiatry and Allied Disciplines*, 1974, *15*, 275–291.
Shaffer, D., and Fisher, P. "The Epidemiology of Suicide in Children and Young Adolescents." *Journal of the American Academy of Child and Adolescent Psychiatry*, 1981, *20*, 545–565.

GIL G. NOAM *is associate professor at Harvard Medical School and the Human Development and Psychology Program, Harvard Graduate School of Education. He is also director of the Hall-Mercer Laboratory of Developmental Psychology and Developmental Psychopathology at Harvard Medical School and McLean Hospital, Belmont, Massachusetts.*

SOPHIE BORST *is clinical psychologist at Curium Academic Center for Child and Adolescent Psychiatry, The Netherlands. She is also research associate at the Hall Mercer Laboratory of Developmental Psychology and Developmental Psychopathology at Harvard Medical School and McLean Hospital.*

A developmental account is given of the role of self-continuity in insulating adolescents against the risks of suicide.

Self-Continuity in Suicidal and Nonsuicidal Adolescents

Michael Chandler

Adolescents attempt suicide at a rate that is wildly in excess of that reported for any other age group (Diekstra and Moritz, 1987; Hanton, 1986; Schneidman, 1985). This chapter is all about finding a developmental means of accounting for this alarming epidemiological fact. The novel idea that I hope to convey here is that this dramatic spiking in the incidence of self-destructive behaviors is linked to the routine difficulties such young persons encounter in working out age-appropriate ways of vouchsafing their own continuity through time. Extending on a set of findings obtained in collaboration with my colleague Lorraine Ball (Ball and Chandler, 1989), I introduce new evidence demonstrating that even temporary loss of the narrative thread of one's personal persistence—a stitch easily dropped in the course of first knitting up one's identity—can leave some adolescents especially vulnerable to a range of self-destructive impulses, against which others remain better insulated

The task of deciphering the meaning of this proposed link between suicide and the problem of diachronic continuity requires first getting clearer about what is ordinarily meant by the notion of self-continuity, and what is generally known about how young persons routinely come to understand the possibility of personal stability when faced with the inevitability of personal change. This chapter is an introduction to these often unfamiliar matters. What justifies this excursion into matters so seemingly remote from the immediate problem of adolescent suicide is that without some such detour into developmental theory, there seems to be little hope of ever explaining the strongly age-graded character of self-destructive acts. After devoting the front half of this chapter to a discussion of these normative matters, I present pertinent evidence of how failures in such self-continuity warranting practices link up to the actual suicidal behaviors of a group of psychiatrically hospitalized adolescents.

NEW DIRECTIONS FOR CHILD DEVELOPMENT, no. 64, Summer 1994 © Jossey-Bass Publishers

Self-Continuity and Its Developmental Vicissitudes

Contemporary philosophers (for example, Harré, 1979; MacIntyre, 1977; Perry, 1976; Rorty, 1976; Wiggins, 1971) and psychological theorists from James (1892) to Erikson (1968) and beyond (for example, Damon and Hart, 1982; Gergen and Gergen, 1983; Guardo and Bohan, 1971; Peevers, 1987) have generally agreed that the concept of self or personhood necessarily presupposes the satisfaction of two constitutive conditions. The first, given considerable prominence in contemporary developmental research on the identity formation process (for example, Damon and Hart, 1982; Guardo and Bohan, 1971; Peevers, 1987), is that in order to qualify as a self, all of the various component parts that together make up the mosaic of one's simultaneously present attributes must be seen to constitute a single synchronically *unified* whole. That is, it has come to be seen as constitutive of what we ordinarily mean by self- or personhood that there be followable reasons as to why the collection of the simultaneously present attributes that are seen to go into making up a single individual all actually cohere or fit together as attributes of one and the same person. It is for such reasons that when the component parts of any self-system somehow fail such tests of coherence, and utterly refuse to be integrated, that we feel obligated to begin talking of indwelling spirits, or multiple personalities, or otherwise imagine that more than one self somehow coexists inside the skin of what would in some other context be taken to be a single unified individual.

The second, much less studied, but no less constitutive feature of bona fide selves is that despite being subjected to the effects of exceptionless change, they must, nevertheless, somehow justify all their various temporally distinct manifestations as alternative expressions of one and the same individual. It is this historical or diachronic aspect of selves that must be conserved somehow across transformations, lest they cease to qualify as persons at all. The importance attached to this necessary aspect of self-continuity arises because it is precisely this quality of persistence that serves to make each of us responsible for our own pasts and invested in our own as yet unrealized futures. Theologians long ago christened the spiritual counterpart of such diachronic self-continuity "numerical identity" in recognition of the fact that, like selves, souls too must depend for their efficacy on being counted only once (Chandler, Boyes, Ball, and Hala, 1986). Without some such accounting scheme Saint Peter, for example, whose job is presumably to keep track of just how many distinct souls are afoot in the world, would obviously have hell to pay. Despite the linchpin role of self-continuity in holding together the successive time slices that together make up the archipelago of the historical self, however, research psychologists have only recently begun to pay the notion of self-continuity any serious heed.

From the point of view of putative owners of selves, the key problem with the necessity of self-continuity lies in the obligation to seek out adequate explanatory means or "warranting practices" that acknowledge those evident personal changes that occur and, at the same time, to render these different ways of being either structurally equivalent or otherwise functionally interchangeable. A self that lacked this quality of persistence, and instead simply winked in and out of existence with every momentary change, would be unrecognizable as an instance of what selves are generally understood to be. Continuity, then, represents a necessary condition over which the term *self* is reasonably allowed to operate (Shotter, 1984), for the reason that a self that is not taken by others to be somehow abiding would be fundamentally nonsensical (Luckman, 1976). Consequentially, if we could not manage to see how our pasts or likely futures are our own, then we would fail in a fundamental way to live up to one of the primary constitutive conditions of selfhood and would cease to be distinct persons in our own and others' eyes.

Although, as Lifton (1974) pointed out, the various argumentative grounds capable of justifying this necessary sense of self-continuity are not commonly part of conscious awareness, they nevertheless underlie and support the tone and quality of one's self-awareness and often do become explicitly available to awareness during crisis points and times of transition (Barclay and Smith, 1990). Consciously available or not, our sense of well-being nevertheless depends on the defensible conviction that we do in fact extend forward and backward in time. At least, that has been the germ of Erikson's (1968) and our own insistence that a sense of diachronic continuity is fundamental to what it means to have or be a self.

If each of us is under an obligation to somehow work out viable means of successfully warranting our beliefs in our own personal persistence, then there is every reason to suppose that as individuals develop, the cognitive complexity or formal adequacy of their self-continuity warranting practices will increase apace. At least, these several expectations served to set in motion my own protracted search, carried out in collaboration with various colleagues (Ball and Chandler, 1989; Chandler and Ball, 1989; Chandler, Boyes, Ball, and Hala, 1986), for possible age-graded changes in the ways that normal young persons actually think about their own personal continuity.

So far, more than one hundred children and adolescents have been extensively interviewed and tested regarding these matters. Our efforts to date have led us to distinguish a total of five distinctive ways in which these subjects have talked about their own persistence through time. Although these continuity-warranting strategies are not seen to structure themselves into the same kind of "strong" stagelike sequences said to characterize the course of operative and moral reasoning development (Kohlberg and Armon, 1984), they nevertheless can be rough-sorted in terms of the adequacy with which they successfully champion personal sameness without also ignoring personal change. Moreover, collateral empirical evidence suggests that increasingly older and more cognitively mature subjects also prefer the more formally adequate of these several continuity-warranting practices. In the following sections, I list and describe these different ways of reasoning about personal sameness, some of which I broadly characterize as *structural* and others as *functional* continuity warrants.

A Typology of Alternative Self-Continuity Warrants

The five alternative ways in which young persons so far have been noted to reason in favor of their own continuous identities are further distinguishable in terms of whether they rest on arguments that are basically structural or functional in character. My use of the term *structural continuity warrants* relies on Barclay and Smith's (1990) "entity" notion of self and has as the common feature the fact that they are meant to vouchsafe one's persistence in the face of change by drawing attention to the presence of one or more structural details of the self that are presumed to somehow stand apart from time, and to go on being identical to themselves despite acknowledged changes in other quarters. Three self-continuity warrants of this structural sort have been identified. These are referred to in this chapter as "simple inclusion," "typological," and "essentialist" warranting strategies.

Functional continuity warrants avoid all such suspect claims about the supposed architectural features of the self that are somehow imagined to be immune to the workings of time. Instead, arguments of this caliber rest their case on claims for various continuity-engendering relational forms that stitch together, into one functional unit, "time slices" of the self. By such lights, an individual inevitably going through various personal changes is nevertheless held to be selfsame if a case can be made that the person one once was and has since become are functionally related. Two such functional arguments have been identified. These different functional approaches roughly parallel the familiar cause-reason distinction and are referred to here as "foundational" and "narrative" warranting strategies.

Each of these five distinct continuity-warranting strategies is based on a different conception of the structure or architecture of the self, and on different assumptions regarding the sorts of changes to which these self-structures are subject (see Table 4.1).

Table 4.1. Typology of Possible Self-Continuity Warrants

Level	Warranting Strategy	Grounds for Continuity	Characterization of the Self	Interpretation of Change
1	Simple inclusion	Structural	Figural collection mosaic of parts	Change is discounted
2	Typological	Structural	Multifaceted typo-logical structure	Change is denied
3	Essentialist	Structural	Unchanging geno-typical core	Change is trivialized
4	Foundational	Relational or functional	Effect or logical implication of a determining past	Determinate change is rationalized
5	Narrative	Relational or functional	Autobiography or narrative center of gravity	Change triggers a hermeneutic rereading of the past

What will become obvious as the discussion proceeds here is that the earlier ways of thinking about selfhood are less adequate to the task of warranting self-continuity than are their successors. However, as I later make clear, it is not so much a running behind developmental schedule with reference to these continuity warrants that characterizes suicidal adolescents as it is that these young persons have somehow fallen completely through the cracks while attempting to navigate between the levels of the various self-warranting practices.

Simple Inclusion Arguments. Claims about personal continuity that fall under the heading of "simple inclusion arguments" all begin with a characterization of the self as a mere mosaic of juxtaposed parts, and a conception of personal change that simply allows new elements to be tacked on, or old parts sloughed off, without consideration for their places within the larger whole. Given such an add-on conception of selfhood and the suffixed changes that it allows, all such bids in favor of self-continuity must necessarily rest on the hope that after each successive landslide of personal change, there will remain at least one atomic fact about one's former identity that can be pointed to as the basis for one's persistence through time. Resting one's case for personal persistence on the fact that, despite other changes, at least one's name, for example, or fingerprints, or street address still remains the same is typical of continuity warrants of this caliber. While better than no sense of personal persistence at all, continuity arguments of this quite primitive sort suffer from the limitation that the whole of one's identity amounts to no more than an arbitrary collage of whatever residual aspects of the self have thus far escaped the ravages of time.

Typological Arguments. The second in this series of increasingly complex continuity-warranting strategies rejects as inadequate all simpler claims that the self is no more than some transient collection of arbitrary parts and substitutes in their place a somewhat better organized typological surface structure, the separate attributes of which are worn much like the fixed facets of some empty polyhedronic shape. An important part of what is accomplished by viewing selves in this way is that what would otherwise necessarily count as evidence of personal change can now be redescribed as merely presentational, as but one of the facets of a self-structure now being showcased at the expense of others that are temporarily thrown into eclipse. Persons who see themselves as having a devil on one shoulder and an angel on the other, both of which alternatively thrust themselves forward from time to time, provide examples of such typological views of self-structure. Change, in this still primitive conception of the self, amounts to little more than a spatial rearrangement of parts (Shotter, 1984) and is thus effectively denied. As such, the continuity-warranting practices that grow out of such typological conceptions of self and change manage to "solve" the problem of personal persistence, but only by writing off real changes as matters of mere appearance.

Essentialist Arguments. Essentialist arguments basically hinge on a genotype-phenotype distinction and are the first in this sequence of progressively more complex structural self-continuity warranting practices to succeed in justifying personal sameness without turning a blind eye to the real changes occurring in the self. Persons who follow this approach tend to characterize the self as a structure with a certain depth, the deeper layers of which are taken to be more central to, and defining of, the true essence of one's unique nature. Given this hierarchical arrangement, change, or at least changes of a certain presumably superficial sort, can be written off easily as mere phenotypical variations while, beneath this changing surface structure, there remains a subterranean core of essential sameness, a rock of persistent selfhood capable of paraphrasing itself in endless superficial variations.

Among the things that are free to vary across different versions of essentialist accounting schemes is a depth-of-processing factor that expresses the relative degree of abstraction at which more peripheral differences are seen to be joined. Toward the shallow end of this continuum are, for example, modest trait concepts such as "artistic" or "athletic," which can serve as nodes that join lower-bound dimensions of possible difference such as interest in the visual as opposed to performing arts, or individual versus team sports. The problem with such essentialist attributes of this middle range is that, while more stable than the transient phenotypical specialties they subsume, these second-order attributes also often change. Many people, for example, only start out being athletic or artistic but are not easily describable in those terms as the years take their toll.

Nearer the opposite pole of this depth-of-processing dimension are more abstract notions such as "personality," or the theological idea of an immaterial, featureless, and immutable "soul." Here, there is danger that some situational bad bounce will cause one to lose his or her immortal soul or suffer some fundamental personality change; but the high cost paid for such insulation is that while personalities, souls, and the like are long on generality, they are short on interpersonal currency or connectedness to the mundane concerns of daily life. Despite wholesale change, I may say, for example, that I persist at being myself because I possess an immutable soul. But this can be dismissed as mere handwaving. In short, essentialist arguments function reliably only when composed at a rather top-lofty level of abstraction that does little real practical work. Clearly, such essentialist claims work best in homogeneous and static societies where everyone agrees about the essential stuff of which persons are thought to be made, but they quickly falter in settings of rapid social change. As Lifton (1974) pointed out, various kinds of symptoms of psychological distress, including suicide, occur more frequently when societies do not manage to share with their younger members those symbols of continuity that allow for "experiential transcendence" and entry into what he called "mythic time." It is also worth mentioning that all essentialist continuity warrants, and in fact all "entity" or structural notions of personal persistence, tend, as Barclay and Smith (1990) observed, to decouple the self from the activities of the whole being, and to promote various unworkable dualistic assumptions about indwelling spirits or other "ghosts in the machine."

Foundational and Narrative Arguments. The functional approaches to the problem of personal persistence that make up the fourth and fifth levels in this proposed typology differ from the arguments just outlined in that they abandon as unrealistic all false hopes that there might exist certain persistent attributes of the self that somehow stand outside of the workings of time. In the place of "shared parts" arguments, advocates of these functional approaches substitute a set of alternative problem-solving strategies. According to these strategies, earlier and later versions of the self exhibit diachronic continuity in that these successive time slices are understood to stand in a certain functional relation to one another that cements them in time.

The key difference that divides foundational and narrative continuity warrants is the order in which those who employ them attempt to move between past and present. Foundational arguments build such relations by reading events from the past to the present, claiming that one persists at being one's own self because the present is the *effect* of which one's ancestral past is the antecedent *cause*. Here, for example, past and present are stitched together because of "the terrible fall I took from the high chair" or "my formative prep-school experience," or, more broadly, because once "two roads diverged in a yellow wood and I took the one less traveled by, and that made all the difference" (Frost, 1955, p. 116). The drawback to all such foundational arguments is their deterministic or fatalistic character. By these lights, the past becomes an inescapable force that succeeds at guaranteeing a certain brand of personal continuity only at the expense of emptying the future of all of its potential for surprise, and denying the possibility of real personal reform.

By contrast, narrative arguments, the second type of functional continuity warrants, attempt a more interpretive form of historiography by reading the relation between past and present from back to front. That is, self-history is seen as a storytelling or narrative enterprise that undertakes to reread the past in light of the present in a struggle to give one's life interpretive meaning (Harré, 1979; Ricoeur, 1983). By these lights, remembered selves must be constantly reedited (Barclay and Smith, 1990); an identity is not a static thing but a configuring of personal events into a historical unity (Pollinghorne, 1988); and self-continuity is the ability to tell a believable story about one's self—a story that possesses what Dennett (1978) called a "narrative center of gravity." Those who successfully employ such narrative approaches succeed not by finding ways of showing successive time slices of one and the same person but rather by altogether avoiding this freeze-frame way of looking at selfhood. From this view, the entire life narrative constitutes the self—a story that must be formed and reformed as the events of one's life unfold.

As implied by their ordered presentation, the five levels of the foregoing typology of possible self-continuity warranting practices are envisaged as forming a loose developmental sequence. While the order in which these different means of explaining oneself are acquired does not conform to some iron law, they are viewed as ordered within a "soft" developmental sequence (Kohlberg and Armon, 1984). What is claimed, then, is that arguments further along in this proposed sequence seriously engage problems overlooked at earlier levels and thus represent formally more adequate solutions to the problem of personal continuity. Simple inclusion arguments, for example, are seen as necessarily immature because they turn a blind eye to any change and stake all claims for personal persistence on isolated attributes, no matter how remote these may be from matters of personal relevance. Typological arguments, by contrast, acknowledge change but ultimately discount it as purely presentational. Essentialist warrants successfully hierchicalize the various attributes of the self and, while fully recognizing the possibility of genuine change, nevertheless trivialize it by pointing to "higher" or "deeper" parts that are seen to provide for the genotypical sameness beneath all such phenotypical variation. Foundational warrants, by contrast, successfully slip the leash on all suspect claims about changeless parts, but only at the expense of a deadening fatalism.

Beyond all reasons why some strategies for warranting self-continuity can be viewed as better, or at least more complex, than others, there is also empirical evidence to suggest that movement through this series is both age-graded and related to other common metrics of cognitive maturity. For example, young adolescents (that is, those under age fifteen) have been shown to rely almost exclusively on simple inclusion and typological structural arguments, whereas those sixteen years or older seem to primarily employ essentialist and functional arguments (Chandler, Boyes, Ball, and Hala, 1986). More generally, reliable correlations on the order of .45 have been observed between chronological age and movement through this five-level sequence. Similarly, there is other evidence (Boyes, 1987) that essentialist arguments, which rely on distinctions between the more and less central features of the self, and Levels 4 and 5 functional arguments are routinely available only to those young persons who also demonstrate proficiency on standard measures of formal operational reasoning.

More generally, these empirical research efforts have demonstrated that questions about personal sameness are live issues in the minds of young persons, that adolescents are quick to discuss their views regarding these matters in some detail, and that what they have to say tends to fit comfortably and without remainder into the five-level typology just outlined. Finally, and most pertinent to the discussion that follows, all of the "normal" children and adolescents so far tested have invariably had at their disposal one or another of these more or less adequate ways of vouchsafing their own personal persistence through time.

Getting from Failure in Self-Continuity to Suicide

The account of self-continuity development just outlined could be correct in all of its particulars without simultaneously making any real contribution whatsoever to our understanding of suicidal behavior. What follows now is an attempt to prove the opposite case by examining how a loss of diachronic continuity might actually pave the way toward such life-threatening assaults on the self. I go about this by providing a preliminary list of reasons why young persons who are unable to find the continuous thread in their own identities might be especially inclined to respond to difficulties or disappointments with attempts on their own lives. Having made these conceptual connections, I then turn attention to a quick survey of other collateral lines of evidence indicating that adolescents in general, and suicidal adolescents in particular, regularly suffer some breakdown in their ability to see themselves as temporarily connected to their own determining pasts and likely futures. The additional business of *empirically* demonstrating such connections in groups of suicidal and nonsuicidal adolescents is addressed in the final section of this chapter.

As with growth processes more generally, a number of things can conceivably go wrong with one's efforts to move toward a mature understanding of the grounds on which continuous or numerical identity must necessarily rest. The most obvious of these is to simply get older without also getting better or more mature at justifying one's persistent identity. That is, one can fall short of sustaining a successful conception of self-continuity simply by failing to make timely developmental progress in updating one's thinking about personal sameness in the face of change. It does not seem particularly odd, for example, to hear six- or seven-year-olds defend their convictions about persistent personal sameness by pressing the point that they have continued to live in the same houses or are still called by the same names. Similar statements from the mouths of young adults, however, obviously seem inappropriately childlike.

While fixations or developmental delays of the foregoing sort may set important restrictions on the kinds of personal change that can be countenanced without confusion, such age-inappropriate approaches to the problem of self-continuity merely tax, rather than repeal, the necessity of those constitutive diachronic connections on which all coherent conceptions of selfhood depend. That is, a sense of self-continuity defended even in childish ways is, nevertheless, still some sort of committed view about one's persistence in time.

Qualitative growth models of the elaborate, discontinuous sort promoted here—models that characterize the path of identity development as progressing through an ordered sequence of increasingly adequate problem-solving strategies—suggest the possibility of still other ways in which continuity-warranting practices can go wrong. One such dangerous prospect is that developmentally earlier ways of solving the self-continuity problem will be discarded as immature before some more adequate alternative is fully in place. That is, growth models, such as that proposed here, leave open the possibility of pathologies arising from awkward or failed transitions from one ontogenetic level to the next. Even during the best of such transitional moments, when both of one's conceptual feet are momentarily off the ground, the self is in some jeopardy of temporarily losing its rootedness in its own past and its grounding in its own prospective future. For such persons, I argue, the usual hedges that are commonly thrown up against momentary self-destructive impulses are dramatically lowered.

At one time or another, most people, it seems, have imagined taking their own lives, often for what later appear to be especially trivial reasons (Rubenstein and others, 1988; Ross, 1985). While nearly everyone has thought about escaping their problems by killing themselves, few ever act on such inclinations, primarily, it must be supposed, because the persons who would be hurt or lost will be them—wonderful them. Viewed in these terms, what needs explaining is not so much the impulse to act in self-destructive ways as the occasional absence of those restraints that lead most of us to abandon such passing suicidal thoughts in favor of a future into which we project our own continued existence. Hence, any serious impediment to seeing oneself as having such a personal future or temporally continuous self would work to rob one of his or her best defenses against suicidal thoughts. From this vantage, suicide attempts that are linked to a loss of personal continuity seem more like senseless drive-by shootings or eerily detached high-altitude bombing missions than actual assaults on a future self in which there is some ongoing personal stake.

To the extent that at least some part of the foregoing account proves correct, it goes a considerable distance toward answering two fundamental questions. The first, already partially addressed above, asks how it is that anyone, at any developmental station, could actually manage to override the otherwise universal impulse to preserve and sustain one's own life (Linehan, Goodstein, Nielsen, and Chiles, 1983). The second is directly concerned with adolescents and asks for reasons that might explain the anomalously high rate of suicide attempts in this age group. That is, while the foregoing remarks were meant to make suicide seem more of a live option, at least for those whose identity problems have already cost them all connection to their own futures, no case has yet been made as to why adolescents demonstrate such losses of self-continuity more often than do persons in other age groups.

The basis for an answer to this puzzle lies in the fact that between the middle school years and young adulthood, the typical young persons whom we have tested commonly work their way through as many as four of five different self-continuity warranting strategies. During each of these transition periods, the prospect exists that these young persons will abandon older and less adequate claims about personal continuity well before anything that could qualify as a more mature alternative is yet in view. In short, if hazards to the self are most often met on the cusp of a transition from one self-continuity warranting strategy to the next, then adolescents who are forever coming to view their sense of self in some new way will thus distinguish themselves as a particularly high-risk group.

During such more or less extended transitional moments, one's sense of temporal connectedness can be easily lost. Without a diachronic framework linking one's past, present, and future, such persons have no more reason to be committed to their own future well-being than they are to the fortunes of a complete stranger. If, during such periods of selflessness, negative circumstances conspire to make one's life of the moment seem intolerable, then suicide becomes a live option lacking in all of its usual serious and sobering personal consequences.

Such a view has a number of decided advantages over competing accounts. By making suicidality the result of a disrupted transitional *state,* rather than some fixed personality *trait,* the transient and nonrecurrent nature of such self-destructive behaviors are better accounted for. By linking suicidal acts to moments of developmental change, reasons are provided as to why such self-destructive behaviors most often occur during periods of developmental transition (puberty, age of retirement, beginning senility, and so on). And, most important, by making provision for the fact that the victim of one's own suicidal acts is, under these special circumstances, experienced as a person numerically distinct from one's self, a way is found of circumventing those natural inhibitions that otherwise operate against acts of self-harm.

Comparison of Continuity Claims of Suicidal and Nonsuicidal Adolescents

In comparison to the more roundabout tasks of explicating the notion of self-continuity and of explaining why failures to maintain such a sense of personal persistence might be conducive to suicide, the job of laying out available evidence concerning how suicidal and nonsuicidal persons differently approach the task of providing reasons for their own continuity is relatively straightforward. Some of the procedural details and early findings of the research program on which I report here have already been presented elsewhere (Ball and Chandler, 1989; Chandler and Ball, 1989; Chandler, Boyes, Ball, and Hala, 1986). Notwithstanding a certain necessary overlap with these earlier reports, three general sorts of things must be considered here. First, some brief account is needed of the particular methods employed for getting at what both suicidal and nonsuicidal adolescents actually believe about their own self-continuity. Next, sufficient normative data must be presented for an adequate understanding of the usual self-continuity warranting practices of ordinary adolescents, and how these change with age and other markers of cognitive development. Finally, new evidence must be presented that complements and extends earlier findings (Ball and Chandler, 1989) that suicidal adolescents are wholly unlike their nonsuicidal age-mates in that they appear to have lost all sense of their own personal persistence through time.

Before going on, however, it is useful to briefly preview the message arising from these research efforts. The interesting point is this: Normal adolescents, even psychiatrically hospitalized but not suicidal adolescents, while differing in the evident maturity or formal complexity of their beliefs about self-continuity, nevertheless succeed in reasoning their way to the conclusion that, despite real changes, they are persistently themselves. That is, despite other important individual differences, including self-reports of depressive affect, nonsuicidal youth of every stripe seem able to successfully count their own pasts and as yet unrealized futures as their own. In sharp contrast, better than four out of every five of the suicidal subjects so far tested completely lack any effective means of warranting their own self-continuity, and so stand stripped of all connections to their pasts or investments in their own future well-being. What is accomplished by this all but complete segregation of suicidal from nonsuicidal subjects is not only the practical promise of an eventual diagnostic instrument powerful enough to overcome the actuarial obstacles associated with the generally low base rate of suicide, but also, and more important, a conceptually coherent means for understanding the high incidence of attempted suicides among adolescents. In a research environment sometimes, reduced to the seemingly circular demonstration that suicidal individuals regularly feel hopeless and depressed, there is enough that appears new here to justify a closer look at the specifics of these methods and results.

Measuring the Presence or Absence of Various Self-Continuity Warranting Practices. As described earlier, the issue of one's own continuous or numerical identity is not ordinarily the sort of matter about which one consciously deliberates. Consequently, some care must be devoted to the job of finding just the right procedural means for bringing out peoples' best thoughts on these usually implicit matters. What was eventually hit upon as a method for directing subjects to these otherwise background considerations was a structured interview that begins by asking about the continuity or lack of continuity in the biographies of various fictional characters chosen from among the literary classics. The kernel idea here is that "character development," as it is commonly understood, amounts to a set of literary devices employed by authors as a way of guaranteeing a certain followable continuity in the lives of storied persons. By pressing for explanations as to how certain familiar fictional characters went on being themselves despite often dramatic changes, we created opportunities for easing subjects into discussions of their own well-guarded and otherwise often inaccessible thoughts about the grounds for their own personal continuity.

The suicidal and nonsuicidal adolescent subjects were first given "Classic Comic Book" versions of Victor Hugo's *Les Miserables* and Charles Dickens's *A Christmas Carol*, and then they were asked to discuss ways in which Jean Valjean and Ebenezer Scrooge were alike and different from themselves at the beginning and end of these stories. After agreeing that both of these stories were about unfolding events in the lives of what they took to be one and the same numerically identical person, they were pressed for detailed explanations of what they understood to be the basis for their strong beliefs in the self-continuity of these story characters. All of these efforts were prodromal to the positing of a parallel set of questions about their own lives, in which subjects were first asked for past and present descriptions of themselves, and then for reasons for believing that they too were continuous, numerically identical persons (for further details regarding these assessment procedures, see Ball and Chandler, 1989).

Almost all of the ordinary and psychiatrically hospitalized adolescents so far tested with these procedures have found the issues at hand to be matters worthy of discussion, and typically they have gone on to offer lengthy replies to questions about their own self-continuity warranting practices. Verbatim transcripts of these accounts have proved to be highly scoreable in terms of the typology of different continuity warrants detailed earlier, and pairs of blind raters generally have been in close agreement as to how such protocols ought to be coded. Finally, and most pertinent to the purposes of this chapter, adolescent subjects have been observed not only to employ each of the five continuity-warranting strategies discussed but also to sometimes throw up their hands in failed attempts to find any personally acceptable means of judging themselves or others as truly continuous in the face of change.

Clues About the Normative Course Followed in Achieving a Mature Sense of Self-Continuity. Data from the approximately one hundred nonhospitalized adolescents between the ages of twelve and eighteen interviewed thus far permit the drawing of a few general conclusions about the usual course of self-continuity development. One of these is that while individual adolescents have been observed to employ each of the five warranting strategies described, simple inclusion (level 1) warrants were generally issued by only the youngest, and narrative (level 5) warrants were employed by only a few of the oldest and most mature of the subjects. The bulk of these typical twelve- to eighteen-year-olds tended to rely instead on typological (level 2), essentialist (level 3), and foundational (level 4) arguments, with progressively older subjects showing a preference for the more complex of these problem-solving strategies. The age-graded nature of these data is reflected in a positive correlation of .45 between age and the maturity of usual warranting practices.

A further set of findings that cross-classify self-continuity warranting practices with Piagetian levels of operativity support the related view that there is a certain predictable relationship between the ways in which young persons think about matters of self-continuity and the ways in which they undertake to solve various less personal cognitive problems. What these data generally suggest is that only adolescents scored as formal operational were also able to make use of essentialist (level 3), foundational (level 4), or narrative (level 5) solutions to the problem of personal sameness in the face of change.

Self-Continuity Warranting Practices of Suicidal and Nonsuicidal Adolescents. An earlier study (Ball and Chandler, 1989) constituted a test of the key expectation that suicidal adolescents would evidence a fundamental disruption in their ability to see themselves as continuous with their own pasts and future selves. This study began with an attempted three-way comparison between thirty suicidal and nonsuicidal psychiatrically hospitalized adolescents and a matched group of their nonhospitalized age-mates. It quickly proved impossible to successfully identify psychiatrically hospitalized adolescents whose medical records were altogether free of references to implicit or explicit threats of suicide. Consequently, a coding system was introduced for rating each subject's medical records in terms of the evident degree of suicidal risk. These data were consequently collapsed to create a "low-risk" and a "high-risk" group. This classification scheme took into account a variety of factors, including suicidal ideation and the recency, number, and degree of lethality of previous suicide attempts. In the end, however, classification in the high-risk group effectively proved to coincide with having been placed on "active suicide precautions" during some part of the then-current period of hospitalization. By contrast, the low-risk group was made up only of persons who were not known to have made such "serious" suicide attempts.

The key finding of this earlier study was that whereas subjects in the low-risk group and their nonhospitalized controls were all found to make use of some more or less mature self-continuity warranting strategy, three out of every four of the high-risk group wholly lacked any means of seeing themselves as connected to their own pasts and futures. In addition, the two high-risk subjects who proved to be exceptions to this general rule were altogether unlike their low-risk counterparts, who had been observed to employ only the most immature of warranting practices. These two "outliers" were found to have especially mature ideas about their own personal persistence (that is, levels 4 and 5), but they were also characterized by various life circumstances that made their own acknowledged future prospects especially bleak. In short, adolescents could be suicidal without also demonstrating problems in self-continuity, but the opposite case did not hold. That is, the combined effect of the several tendencies evident within this earlier data set was to create a picture of self-continuity problems as essentially unique markers of suicidal behavior. It is noteworthy that various clinically based ratings of depression and the responses of these subjects to Beck's Hopelessness Scale failed to significantly differentiate these high- and low-risk groups.

In the interim, from the time that the protocols originally reported by Ball and Chandler (1989) were collected, a dozen new clinical cases and an equal number of control cases have been added to this accumulating data set. Among the new hospitalized subjects, five were coded as high risk and seven as low risk. In keeping with the pattern set by their high-risk counterparts in the earlier study, none of these new highly suicidal subjects evidenced any working mechanisms for warranting self-continuity through time. Similarly, while all but one of the new low-risk hospitalized subjects were again found to possess some method of warranting their own continuity, in keeping with the earlier findings, all of these were of the less-complex simple inclusion (level 1) and typological (level 2) variety. Finally, the twelve new control cases evenly distributed themselves, as did those described by Ball and Chandler (1989), with somewhat more than half employing either essentialist (level 3), foundational (level 4), or narrative (level 5) warranting strategies. Again, no nonhospitalized subject responded in a way that failed to find an acceptable means of warranting self continuity.

Table 4.2 combines these new cases with those previously reported by Ball and Chandler (1989). As can be seen, more than 80 percent of the high-risk

Table 4.2. Type of Continuity Warrant by Suicidal Status

	Type of Warrant		
Suicidal Status	None	Simple Inclusion or Typological	Essentialist or Functional
High risk	14 (.82)	1 (.06)	2 (.12)
Low risk	3 (.13)	18 (.78)	2 (.09)
Control	0	16 (.40)	25 (.60)

Note: Table figures are *N*'s, with cell percentages in parentheses; total *N* = 81, high-risk *N* = 17, low-risk *N* = 23, control *N* = 41.

subjects so far tested wholly lacked any means of warranting their own self-continuity, whereas this was true for 13 percent of the low-risk hospitalized subjects and none of the nonhospitalized controls.

This evidence, old and new, is taken as a strong demonstration of the theoretical and practical promise of the present attempt to understand the anomalously high rate of suicide attempts by adolescents as a partial consequence of the difficulties such young persons commonly experience in searching out some basis for their own self-continuity or numerical identity. Should future research continue to support this conclusion, we will have come a crucial distance toward better understanding the strong relation between suicide attempts and age. Perhaps more important, these results also point the way to certain interventions that might help young persons see their way through difficult transitions en route toward a more mature sense of diachronic self-continuity.

References

Ball, L., and Chandler, M. "Identity Formation in Suicidal and Nonsuicidal Youth: The Role of Self-Continuity." *Development and Psychopathology*, 1989, *1*, 257–275.

Barclay, C., and Smith, T. "Autobiographical Remembering and Self-Composing." *International Journal of Personal Construct Psychology*, 1990, *35*, 59–65.

Boyes, M. "Epistemic Development and Identity Formation in Adolescence." Unpublished doctoral dissertation, University of British Columbia, 1987.

Chandler, M., and Ball, L. "Continuity and Commitment: A Developmental Analysis of Identity Formation Process in Suicidal and Non-Suicidal Youth." In H. Bosma and S. Jackson (eds.), *Coping and Self-Concept in Adolescence*. New York: Springer-Verlag, 1989.

Chandler, M., Boyes, M., Ball, S., and Hala, S. "The Conservation of Selfhood: Children's Changing Conceptions of Self-Continuity." In T. Honess and K. Yardley (eds.), *Self and Identity: Individual Change and Development*. New York: Routledge & Kegan Paul, 1986.

Damon, W., and Hart, D. "The Development of Self-Understanding from Infancy Through Adolescence." *Child Development*, 1982, *53*, 841–864.

Dennett, D. *Brainstorms*. Hassocks, N.J.: Harvester Press, 1978.

Diekstra, R., and Moritz, B. "Suicidal Behavior Among Adolescents: An Overview." In R. Diekstra and K. Hawton (eds.), *Suicide in Adolescents*. Dordrecht, Netherlands: Martinus Nijhoff, 1987.

Erikson, E. H. *Identity, Youth, and Crisis*. New York: Norton, 1968.

Frost, R. "The Road Not Taken." In M. L. Rosenthal and A.S.M. Smith (eds.), *Exploring Poetry*. New York: Macmillan, 1955.

Gergen, K., and Gergen, M. "Narratives of the Self." In T. R. Sarbin and K. E. Schebe (eds.), *Minnesota Symposia on Child Psychology.* Vol. 15. Hillsdale, N.J.: Erlbaum, 1983.

Guardo, C. J., and Bohan, J. B. "Development of a Sense of Self-Identity in Children." *Child Development,* 1971, *42,* 1909–1921.

Hanton, K. *Suicide and Attempted Suicide Among Children and Adolescents.* Newbury Park, Calif.: Sage, 1986.

Harré, R. *Social Being: A Theory for Social Psychology.* Oxford, England: Blackwell, 1979.

James, W. *Psychology: The Briefer Course.* Troy, Mo.: Holt, Rinehart & Winston, 1892.

Kohlberg, L., and Armon, C. "Three Types of Stage Models Used in the Study of Adult Development." In M. L. Commons, F. A. Richards, and C. Armon (eds.), *Beyond Formal Operations: Late Adolescent and Adult Cognitive Development.* Vol. 1. New York: Praeger, 1984.

Lifton, R. *Living and Dying.* New York: Praeger, 1974.

Linehan, M., Goodstein, J., Nielsen, S., and Chiles, J. "Reasons for Staying Alive When You Are Thinking of Killing Yourself: The Reasons for Living Inventory." *Journal of Consulting and Clinical Psychology,* 1983, *51,* 276–286.

Luckman, T. "Personal Identity as an Evolutionary and Historical Problem." In M. von Cranach (ed.), *Human Ethology.* Cambridge, England: Cambridge University Press, 1976.

MacIntyre, A. "Epistemological Crisis, Dramatic Narrative, and the Philosophy of Science." *The Monist,* 1977, *60* (4), 453–472.

Peevers, B. H. "The Self as Observer of the Self: A Developmental Analysis of the Subjective Self." In T. Honess and K. M. Yardley (eds.), *Self and Identity.* London: Routledge & Kegan Paul, 1987.

Perry, J. "The Importance of Being Identical." In A. O. Rorty (ed.), *The Identities of Persons.* Berkeley: University of California Press, 1976.

Polkinghorne, C. *Narrative Knowing and the Human Sciences.* Albany: State University of New York Press, 1988.

Ricoeur, P. "Can Fiction Narratives Be True?" *Analecta Husserliana,* 1983, *14,* 3–19.

Rorty, A. O. *The Identities of Persons.* Berkeley: University of California Press, 1976.

Ross, C. P. "Teaching Children Facts of Life and Death: Suicide Prevention in the Schools." In M. L. Peck, N. L. Faberow, and R. E. Litman (eds.), *Youth Suicide.* New York: Springer, 1985.

Rubenstein, J. L., Heeren, T., Housman, D., Rubin, C., and Stechler, G. "Suicidal Behavior in 'Normal' Adolescents: Risk and Protective Factors." Paper presented at the biennial meeting of the Society for Research in Adolescence, Alexandria, Va., Mar. 1988.

Schneidman, E. S. *Definition of Suicide.* New York: Wiley, 1985.

Shotter, J. *Social Accountability and Selfhood.* Oxford, England: Blackwell, 1984.

Wiggins, D. *Identity and Spatio-Temporal Continuity.* Oxford, England: Blackwell, 1971.

MICHAEL CHANDLER is professor and coordinator of graduate training in developmental psychology at the University of British Columbia, Vancouver, Canada.

Empirical evidence is presented for a model of risk factors contributing to suicidal ideation among a normative sample of adolescents as well as a clinical sample of inpatients with depression.

Psychosocial Risk Factors Contributing to Adolescent Suicidal Ideation

Susan Harter, Donna B. Marold

The incidence of suicide among adolescents has tripled in recent decades, leading to efforts to identify the determinants of this major mental health threat to our youth (see Eisenberg, 1980; McIntosh, 1991; Pfeffer, 1986, 1988; Alcohol, Drug Abuse, and Mental Health Administration, 1989). As McIntosh (1991) noted, among fifteen- to twenty-four-year-olds there has been an increase of approximately 200 percent from the mid 1950s to the early 1980s. In 1953, the suicide rate within this age group was 4.4 per 100,000, compared to 13.1 in 1986.

Several broad classes of risk factors implicated in depression and suicidal behaviors, including biological precursors, epidemiological correlates, and social-psychological stressors, have captured the attention of researchers. Our own research group has been particularly committed to an examination of the social-psychological class of risk factors. A constellation of social-psychological correlates that predicts suicidal behavior includes depressed affect, poor self-concept in particular domains, discrepancy between real and ideal selves, low self-esteem, hopelessness, and lack of social support.

From a developmental perspective, these particular risk factors become increasingly salient as one moves into adolescence (see Emery, 1983). Self-awareness, self-consciousness, introspectiveness, and preoccupation with one's self-

---

The research described here was supported by a grant from the W. T. Grant Foundation awarded to both authors. We thank the personnel and adolescents at Flood Middle School, Rangeview High School, and Columbine Psychiatric Hospital for their cooperation in making this research possible. Inquiries should be sent to the first author at the Department of Psychology, University of Denver, 2155 S. Race St., Denver, CO 80208.

image dramatically increase (see review by Harter, 1990). Self-esteem becomes more vulnerable (Rosenberg, 1979, 1986), and adolescents become more aware of the relationship among self-esteem, social support, and depressed affect (Harter, Marold, and Jackson, 1991). With regard to the support system, the impact of peer support increases dramatically (Brown, 1990; Savin-Williams and Berndt, 1990). Although young adolescents are beginning to make bids for autonomy from parents, they are nevertheless struggling to remain connected (Cooper, Grotevant, and Condon, 1983; Grotevant and Cooper, 1986; Steinberg, 1990), and thus parent support continues to be critical.

Depressive symptomatology increases in adolescence (see Carlson and Cantwell, 1982; Rutter, Izard, and Read, 1985; Sroufe and Rutter, 1985; Shaffer, 1985), and certain associated features such as hopelessness take on increasing importance since they require a level of cognitive functioning that is not completely developed in younger children (Carlson and Garber, 1986; Kendall, Cantwell, and Kazdin, 1989; Rutter, 1988; Shaffer, 1985). Finally, the incidence of suicidal behaviors increases dramatically during adolescence (Carlson and Cantwell, 1982; Cantor, 1987; Hawton, 1986; McIntosh, 1991; Pfeffer, 1988; Shaffer, 1985).

While there is a growing body of findings on the correlates of suicidal behaviors, relatively little attention has been directed toward the development of theory-based models that identify risk factors representing the antecedents as well as mediators of suicidal behaviors. As Spirato, Brown, Overholser, and Fritz (1989) observed, we are particularly in need of models that consider antecedent stresses such as family, peer, and school problems, and that include emotional and cognitive states (for example, depression and hopelessness) that may mediate outcomes such as suicidal behaviors.

Moreover, recently it has been urged that the field take seriously the study of suicidal behavior and its correlates in *normative* populations of young adolescents (Garrison, 1989). Investigators have demonstrated the fruitfulness of examining the prevalence and antecedents of suicidal behaviors among normative populations, including college students (Bonner and Rich, 1987; Rudd, 1989), high school students (Smith and Crawford, 1986), and preadolescent students (Pfeffer, Lipkins, Plutchik, and Mizruchi, 1988). Research comparing clinical and nonclinical control or comparison groups has also been conducted (Maris, 1991; Pfeffer, 1989; Noam and Borst, this volume). However, the period of early adolescence has received relatively little empirical attention.

Thus, a major goal of our research has been to develop a model of psychosocial factors that put young adolescents at risk for suicidal ideation. Like many investigators, we become interested in the general question of what provokes many among our youth to even consider terminating their lives. What cognitive and socioemotional processes conspire to convince an adolescent that life is not worth living? What role do self-representations play in this intrapsychic plot that has such a potentially tragic outcome? What features of the adolescent's socialization history cause one to question one's worth as a person, and the worth of one's life?

Specifically, we extended our earlier normative research on the determinants and consequences of global self-worth. Our previous efforts have provided evidence for a model in which competence in domains deemed important and peer and parent social support impact a depression composite that is composed of self-esteem, affect (cheerful to depressed), and general hopelessness (Harter, 1986, 1990). More recently, we have addressed the issue of whether this depression composite might, in turn, function as a mediator of suicidal ideation in young adolescents. In this chapter, we, first, review the evidence for the postulated links in the model and then share our own findings on the best-fitting model for adolescents. We then present findings comparing our normative sample to a clinical sample of adolescent inpatients with psychiatric diagnoses of depression. Next, we examine the use of self-report measures in identifying adolescents at risk. Finally, we discuss the issue of general models versus the identification of subgroups of adolescents with different pathways to, and profiles of, depressive symptomatology.

Evidence for the Model

There is considerable evidence of the relationships postulated in our model, coming both from other theorists and investigators as well as from our own laboratory.

Relationship Between Depression and Suicidal Behaviors. There is ample evidence that depressive reactions are linked to suicidal behaviors in normative as well as clinical samples of adolescents (for example, Baumeister, 1990; Berman, 1991; Carlson and Cantwell, 1982; Hammen, 1992; Pfeffer, 1986; Shaffer, 1985; Smith and Crawford, 1986). As Pfeffer (1986) noted, depression distinguishes many suicidal adolescents from those who are nonsuicidal, a conclusion that our own findings also support. Of particular relevance to our model is previous evidence revealing that depression appears most directly related to suicidal ideation (Velez and Cohen, 1988).

Hopelessness and Suicidal Behaviors. Hopelessness and helplessness are also factors predisposing individuals to suicidal behaviors as well as powerful correlates of depression (Asarnow, Carlson, and Guthrie, 1987; Baumeister, 1990; Beck, 1975; Beck, Kovacs, and Weissman, 1975; Pfeffer, 1989; Schneidman, 1991; Seligman, 1975; Topol and Reznikoff, 1982). In our own work, we have found it fruitful to distinguish *general* helplessness, the overall perception that one's future appears uncompromisingly bleak, from specific feelings of hopelessness. A more specific sense of hopelessness may be linked to deficiencies in the self (for example, "There is no way I will ever be able to look the way I want to" or "I'll just never be able to get good grades") or to lack of support from others (for example, "There is nothing that will make my parents love me"). Thus, some adolescents are hopeless about changing themselves in areas where they desperately seek success. Others are hopeless about ever garnering the support of the significant adults or peers in their life. Still others are hopeless about both.

Link Between Self-Esteem and Depression. Recent theory and research has placed increasing emphasis on cognitions that give rise to, or accompany, depression. Cognitions involving the self have found particular favor. There is clear historical precedent for including negative self-evaluations as one of a constellation of symptoms experienced in depression, beginning with Freud's ([1917] 1968) observations of the low self-esteem displayed by adults suffering from depressive disorders. Researchers within the psychoanalytic tradition continue to afford low self-esteem a central role in depression (Bibring, 1953; Blatt, 1974). More recently, a number of theorists who have addressed the manifestations of depression in children and adolescents, as well as in adults, have focused on cognitive components involving the self. Attention has been drawn to the role of self-deprecatory ideation in depression (Baumeister, 1990; Beck, 1975; Hammen, 1992; Hammen and Goodman-Brown, 1990; Kovacs and Beck, 1977, 1986), to attributional style (Abramson, Seligman, and Teasedale, 1986; Nolen-Hoeksema, Girgus, and Seligman, 1986; Seligman, 1975), and to sociocognitive influences as well as self-discrepancies (Baumeister, 1990; Kaslow, Rehm, and Siegel, 1984; McCauley, Mitchell, Burke, and Moss, 1988; Pyszcynski and Greenberg, 1987).

In our own studies (see Harter, 1990), we consistently find that among older children and adolescents, self-esteem is highly related to affect along a continuum of cheerful to depressed, corroborating the findings of other research (Beck, 1975; Kaslow, Rehm, and Siegel, 1984). Older children and adolescents within our normative samples who report low self-esteem consistently report depressed affect (Renouf and Harter, 1990). Moreover, among inpatient adolescents with psychiatric diagnoses of depression, we have also found a powerful link between self-esteem and self-reported depressed affect. Among those reporting depressed affect, 80 percent also report low self-esteem.

Role of Social Support. Although it is clear that depression, hopelessness, and low self-esteem are intimately related and may be proximal causes of suicidal behavior, it behooves us to ask what provokes adolescents to feel hopeless, depressed, and unworthy. Lack of social support appears to be one such cause. Our own framework is consistent with the growing literature on the function of social support, not only as a direct source of self-esteem and adjustment (see Barrera, 1988; Cohen and Wills, 1985; Furman, 1989; Sroufe, 1983; Sroufe and Rutter, 1985) but as a buffer, inoculating children against the potentially detrimental effects of negative life events (see Barrera, 1988; Cohen and Wills, 1985; Garmezy and Rutter, 1985; Sandler, Miller, Short, and Wolchik, 1989; Rutter, 1987, 1989).

In developing our original model of the determinants of global self-esteem, we were drawn to the formulation of Cooley (1902), who focused on the impact of social support. In postulating that the origins of self-esteem were primarily social in nature, Cooley adopted the metaphor of the "looking glass self." The self was constructed by casting one's gaze into the social mirror to ascertain the opinions of significant others toward the self. These reflected appraisals of others were then internalized as the self. Thus, if others hold the self in high regard, one's own sense of self-esteem will be high. Conversely, if others display little regard for the self, the incorporation of these negative opinions will have a crippling effect on self-esteem.

A growing body of research reveals that lack of social support is also intimately related to depression, which may in turn provoke suicidal behaviors. For example, failure to obtain peer support has been suggested as a major factor in the suicidal reactions of adolescents (Hawton, Cole, and O'Grady, 1982; Jacobs, 1971; Motto, 1984; Myers, Burke, and McCauley, 1985; Pfeffer, Newcorn, and Kaplan, 1988; Pfeffer, Plutchik, and Mizruchi, 1983; Shaffer, 1985). Lack of support may take the form of the loss or threatened loss of a boyfriend or girlfriend, interpersonal conflict with peers, social isolation, and lack of tolerance for aloneness.

Problems in relationships with parents as well as peers contribute to adolescent suicidal behaviors. For example, Topol and Reznikoff (1982) reported that suicidal adolescents, in comparison to control subjects, acknowledged that they were less likely to have a close, supportive confidant, and that parents were particularly unavailable. Other studies also reveal that suicide attempters typically view their parents as nonsupportive, rejecting, or indifferent to their needs (Goldney, 1985; Pfeffer, 1989).

Depressive reactions, ushering in the potential for suicidal behaviors, are frequently driven by the intense loss of a significant relationship, an analysis with long-standing roots within the Freudian tradition. Some researchers have built on the attachment theory perspective, highlighting the context of interpersonal relatedness (Gotlib and Hammen, 1993) and the implications of the loss of connectedness (Cicchetti and Schneider-Rosen, 1986; Cummings and Cicchetti, 1990). Others have developed sequential models in which the loss of a significant relationship triggers depression, loss of self-esteem, and the potential for suicidal behaviors (Baumeister, 1990; Pyszcynski and Greenberg, 1987). For example, in Pyszcynski and Greenberg's (1987) self-awareness theory, the loss of, or rejection by, a significant other not only triggers a depressive reaction but leads to loss of self-esteem, to the extent that the particular significant other represented a central source of one's feelings of worth.

In our own research (Renouf and Harter, 1990), we have asked young adolescents to describe the most depressing event in the prior year. The majority of the causes involve loss of support through the death of a significant other, separation (for example, divorce, a significant other moved away, or a breakup), interpersonal conflict, or rejection. Moreover, adolescents citing such causes also revealed that their depressive reactions were followed by a decrease in self-esteem.

Effects of Negative Self-Evaluations. The pernicious effect of self-deprecatory ideation on depressive reactions was noted earlier, in highlighting the link between low self-esteem and depression. In fact, certain theorists (for example, Baumeister, 1990) have suggested that depression, coupled with subsequent suicidal behavior, represents an attempt to escape from the self, to put an end to painful self-cognitions that cannot be altered. In elucidating the "ten commandments of suicide," Schneidman (1991) noted that the common stimulus in suicide is intolerable psychological pain.

In addressing the effects of negative self-evaluations, we relied heavily on the formulation of William James (1892), who sought to unravel the antecedents of self-esteem. For James, self-esteem is predicted by the ratio of one's successes to one's pretensions. James contended that individuals do not scrutinize their every action or attribute. Rather, one selectively attends to performance in domains of importance, arenas of one's life in which one has aspirations to succeed. Thus, if one evaluates oneself as competent in domains where one aspires to excel, high self-esteem will be conferred. Conversely, if one falls short of one's ideals, if one falters in domains where one aspires to success, low self-esteem will unfortunately ensue.

It is critical to appreciate that, from a Jamesian perspective, lack of competence in domains deemed unimportant to the self will not adversely affect self-esteem. For example, one may judge oneself to be unathletic; however, if athletic prowess is not an aspiration, such lack of competence will not erode one's self-esteem. Individuals with high self-esteem, therefore, are equipped with self-protective armor allowing them to discount the importance of domains in which they lack ability. Conversely, individuals with low self-esteem appear more defenseless in that they are unable to devalue success in domains of demonstrated or perceived incompetence. For James, therefore, one's cognitive evaluation of adequacy in light of one's aspirations is the cornerstone on which self-esteem is constructed.

Model of Psychosocial Risk Factors Leading to Adolescent Suicidal Ideation

Based on the theoretical legacies of James and Cooley, we have identified two major classes of antecedents. The first, from James, is composed of self-perceptions of competence or adequacy across five domains of importance: scholastic competence, behavioral conduct, physical appearance, peer likability, and athletic competence. The second, derived from Cooley, is composed of support in the form of approval from parents and peers. With regard to both competence or adequacy and support, adolescents also indicate how hopeless they feel about becoming competent or obtaining support.

These antecedents predict that low self-esteem, depressed affect, and general hopelessness are highly related to one another (r's between .70 and .80). As a result, we have created a "depression composite" composed of these three constructs. The creation of this composite was not merely a statistical solution, given the strong interrelationships among these constructs. Rather, low self-esteem, depressed affect, and general hopelessness all appear to be critical to the identification of individuals at risk for clinical depression and suicidal behaviors. Thus, a low score on the depression composite constitutes a psychological red flag that may be of diagnostic significance. The last construct in our model is suicidal ideation, based on the assumption that the depression composite acts as a powerful mediator of suicidal thinking.

The sequential model depicted in Figure 5.1 provides an excellent fit to our data on young adolescents (see Harter, Marold, and Whitesell, 1992, for the details of model testing). Thus, if an adolescent feels that he or she is inadequate in the domains of appearance and peer likability, domains that adolescents rate as important to the self and to peers, the adolescent typically will also report low peer support. Inadequacy in these domains as well as lack of peer support both provoke the personally devastating combination of low self-esteem, depressed affect, and general hopelessness. As Figure 5.1 also depicts, perceptions of scholastic incompetence as well as negative evaluations of one's behavioral conduct precipitate parent disapproval, leading to low scores on the depression composite. The constellation of low self-esteem, depressed affect, and hopelessness, in turn, drives many to consider suicide as a solution, which we speculate is a form of escape from painful cognitions and affects concerning the inadequacy of the self and the disapproving reactions of others.

Recently, we have demonstrated that this model provides an equally good fit among older adolescents, from a large normative sample of ninth- through twelfth-grade high school students. From a developmental perspective, one is typically on the alert for the demonstration of age-related differences in behavior. However, of equal importance is the identification of relationships that are robust across given portions of the life span. Of particular interest among the high school data was the finding that the path from parent social support to the depression composite was slightly more direct than that for the middle-school subjects. This is noteworthy given the common assumption that the impact of parents wanes as one moves through adolescence, in the face of the increasing importance of peer culture. Our results do not support such a contention. Parents' influences continue to be critical.

The efficacy of our model is illustrated by the following poignant self-disclosure by one of the seventeen-year-olds in our normative sample:

I look in the mirror and most days I don't like what I see, I don't like how I look, I don't like myself as a person. So I get depressed, bummed out. Plus, my family has rejected me and that makes me feel pretty lousy about myself. My mother is really on my case because I'm not living up to what she wants me to be. If I get A's in school, she's nice and is proud of me, but if I don't, she doesn't approve of me; you could say how she treats me is conditional on how I do. Mostly she tells me I'm a failure, and I'm beginning to believe it. Doing well in school has always been important to me, but now I feel like I'll never amount to anything. There's no way I'll ever be able to please her, it's pretty hopeless. I don't get much support from other kids either. I probably never will because I'm an introvert, I don't even try to make friends. So a lot of the time I get depressed, so bummed out that I often think about just killing myself. Life is worthless. But so is death. So what's the use?

Figure 5.1. General Model of Psychosocial Risk Factors for Adolescents

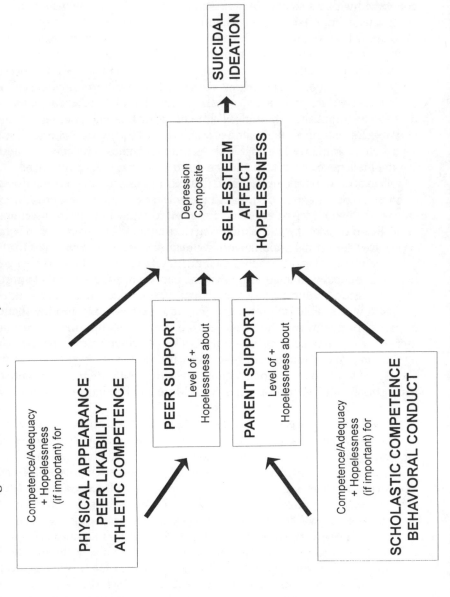

Our adolescent narrator identifies each of the features in our sequential process model predisposing him to thoughts of suicide. He is dissatisfied with his appearance, his outer self, leading him to denigrate himself as a person, to question his essential worth as a human being. As an introvert, he questions his likability, acknowledging that he receives little support from peers. He is dissatisfied with his scholastic performance, a domain that he values, as does his mother, who considers him a failure, a view that he has begun to internalize, leading him to devalue himself further. It is noteworthy that he labels her reactions as "conditional" (a concept to which we next turn), reactions that further contribute to his feelings of worthlessness. This constellation of precursors ushers in very intense feelings of depression and hopelessness. The toll exacted is tortuous, as he wrestles with the question of whether to kill himself and with the uselessness of both his life and death.

The concept of conditionality of support is vital. The troubled adolescent just quoted complained that "if I get A's in school, she's [mother] nice and is proud of me, but if I don't, she doesn't approve of me; you could say how she treats me is conditional on how I do." Other adolescents in both our normative and clinical samples also voiced their distress over the fact that parents only display their support if the adolescent meets typically high, and seemingly unreasonable, parental standards of performance. In addition, adolescents identified the contingencies governing peer support, namely, that approval from age-mates is only forthcoming if one meets certain standards of behavior, attitudes, dress, and so on. Thus, not only level but also type of support have emerged as potential predictors in our network of constructs.

Following the descriptive lead of our adolescent interviewees, we crafted items (Marold, 1987) that contrasted such conditionality to unconditional positive regard (see Rogers and Dymond, 1954) in which one is loved or supported for who one is as a person, not for whether one fulfills the expectations of others. Our findings (Harter, Marold, and Whitesell, 1992) demonstrate the damaging effects of conditionality on self-esteem. The more conditional the perceived support, the lower one's self-esteem.

Conditionality seems to undermine self-esteem because it does not validate or signify approval of the self; it does not communicate genuine support for who one is as a person. Rather, it serves to specify behavioral contingencies through which one can please parents or peers. As such, it is undoubtedly interpreted as controlling, rather than enhancing (see Deci and Ryan, 1985). Moreover, conditional support not only undermines one's self-esteem but also contributes to depressed mood as well as general hopelessness.

Conditionality of parent support, combined with moderate to low levels of support, has other negative effects on the self-system as well. Specifically, we have recently turned our attention to the construct of true- versus false-self behavior among adolescents, that is, the extent to which one feels one can or cannot be the "real me inside" (Bleiberg, 1984; Broughton, 1981; Selman, 1980; Winnicott, 1965). Those adolescents reporting relatively low levels of support that was conditional also reported hopelessness about ever obtaining support, which in turn caused them to engage in false-self behavior (Harter, Marold, and Whitesell, 1992). Given that whatever support they received was conditional on meeting the parents' expectations, it is understandable why such adolescents felt hopeless about obtaining approval for their true-self behavior, which in turn appeared to provoke them to engage in false-self behavior in an attempt to appease their parents.

Comparisons of Normative and Clinical Samples

Recently, we turned our attention to a clinical inpatient sample of sixty adolescents (twenty-three males and thirty-seven females), ages thirteen to sixteen, all of whom had primary psychiatric diagnoses of depression (*DSM*-III-R criteria): major depression (thirty-eight), dysthymia (twenty), adjustment disorder with mixed emotional features (one), and bipolar disorder (one). In addition, twenty-seven of the subjects had an Axis-II diagnosis (personality disorders). An examination of the mean scores provides a compelling look at how the dynamics in the model were operative among the clinical sample. Given our interest in illuminating factors related to suicidal ideation, we compared three groups, matched on age and gender: (1) adolescents within our clinical sample who reported relatively high levels of suicidal ideation, (2) adolescents within our normative sample who reported comparable levels of suicidal ideation, and (3) adolescents within our normative sample who reported the absence of suicidal ideation.

Table 5.1 presents the mean scores for the three groups on critical variables in the model, as well as for conditionality and true- versus false-self behaviors. All dimensions were scored on a 4-point scale. Low scores represent the more negative outcome (for example, low competence/adequacy, low support, conditionality of support, hopelessness, false-self behavior, greater depressed affect). As anticipated, those adolescents in the nonsuicidal normative sample had scores that were mostly very positive. They felt relatively adequate, they reported support from parents and peers, they were hopeful about the continuation of such support, parent approval was perceived as unconditional, they were able to be their true selves, and their depression composite scores indicate that they were cheerful and hopeful and felt esteem for the self.

What is particularly striking, however, is the similarity of the patterns for the normative subgroup reporting suicidal ideation and the clinical subgroup reporting suicidal ideation. On two of the domains most predictive of the depression composite, scholastic competence and physical appearance, both groups had comparable scores that were well below the mean for the nonsuicidal normative group. Moreover, their scores on hopelessness about ever becoming more scholastically competent or good-looking were also relatively low. Both the normative and the clinical group of adolescents who acknowledged suicidal ideation also reported lower levels of parent support and more hopelessness about obtaining such support, greater conditionality of parent

Table 5.1. Comparison of Normative and Clinical
Samples on Key Constructs

Construct	Nonsuicidal Normative	Suicidal Normative	Suicidal Clinical
Scholastic competence	3.00	2.57	2.43
Hopelessness/Scholastics	3.41	2.89	2.82
Appearance	2.70	2.16	1.77
Hopelessness/Appearance	3.16	2.54	2.72
Parent support	3.35	2.74	2.85
Conditionality/Parent support	3.22	2.65	2.77
Hopelessness/Parent support	3.25	2.60	2.76
True/False self with parents	3.22	2.56	2.62
Classmate support	3.05	2.76	2.58
Hopelessness/Classmate support	3.27	2.88	2.85
True/False self with classmates	3.30	2.90	2.75
Depression composite	3.31	2.52	2.16

Note: Figures are mean scores on a scale ranging from a low of 1 (highly negative outcome) to a high of 4 (highly positive outcome).

support, as well as more false self behavior with parents compared to the nonsuicidal normative sample. The patterns are similar for peer support, in that both of the suicidal ideation groups reported comparably lower levels of approval from classmates, greater hopelessness about obtaining such support, and more false-self behavior compared to the nonsuicidal normative group.

With regard to the depression composite, the nonsuicidal normative group scored significantly higher than either of the suicidal ideation groups, who were both at or below the midpoint of 2.5. The clinical sample is understandably lower than the normative suicidal ideation group, given that they had psychiatric diagnoses of depression. Thus, what is striking is that the self-report measures we have developed have allowed us to identify a group of adolescents within a normative sample who appeared to be at risk.

Use of Self-Report Measures in the Evaluation of Dimensions of Depression

The findings that those youth within a normative sample who acknowledged high levels of suicidal ideation also reported perceptions of self and other that were comparable to those of an inpatient sample, clinically diagnosed as depressed, argue for the utility of self-report measures as screening instruments within the school setting. Increasingly, those in the field of psychopathology in general and depression in particular have underscored the need to include self-report measures as supplements to clinical interview and therapy material. Rutter (1989) urged that we employ self-report measures in addition to the more standard psychiatric diagnostic procedures. He noted that it is particularly desirable to include a child questionnaire in any screening for disorders that may involve affective components. Kazdin (1981, 1990) also argued that self-report measures are particularly useful for many of the symptoms of depression that involve the subjective experience of the child or adolescent. In a similar vein, Plutchik and Conte (1989) claimed that self-report scales can provide information about emotions at least as reliably and validly as can clinicians' interviews. Pfeffer, noted for her studies of depression and suicidal behaviors, also urged that investigators employ self-report procedures, emphasizing the importance of obtaining the "youngster's perception of the adequacy in social adjustment with respect to role function in school, at work, and with peers and family" (1988, p. 653). The importance of self-report measurement is further documented in La Greca's (1990) edited volume, which contains chapters on the use of self-report measures in the assessment of depression, other affects such as fears and anxieties, social status and competence, and self-concept. Moreover, the Alcohol, Drug Abuse, and Mental Health Administration (1989) has made a critical call for screening instruments that are sensitive (correctly identifying almost all the young people at high risk), specific (accurately differentiating high-risk youth from those who are at normal or low risk), inexpensive, easily administered, and easily scored and interpreted.

Although we do not see the instruments that we have developed in this research program as alternatives to interviews or standard diagnostic procedures, we nevertheless feel that their utility as screening instruments to identify adolescents potentially at risk has been demonstrated. With regard to the identification of adolescents at risk for suicidal behaviors, our suicidal ideation subscale on the Dimensions of Depression Profile (Harter, Nowakowski, and Marold, 1989) holds promise. For example, we selected a subgroup of adolescents from our normative sample who had reported suicidal ideation and administered Pfeffer's (1986) standardized interview that identifies five levels of suicidal behavior (in order of least to most severe): (1) *no suicidal ideation/behavior:* "Have not thought about committing suicide or hurting yourself," (2) *suicidal ideation:* "Have said to yourself or told someone else that you have thought about killing yourself," (3) *suicidal threat:* "Have told someone about a plan in which you might kill yourself, like threatening to jump off a bridge, or buying or stealing a gun or medication," (4) *mild attempt:* "Have hurt yourself in a way that you knew would not result in your death and did not require a lot of attention," and (5) *serious attempt:* "Have hurt yourself in a way that could have resulted in your death and did need or could have needed a lot of medical attention."

The findings were as follows: None of the twenty-four students reporting suicidal ideation on our scale fell in the Level 1 (no suicidal ideation/behavior) category. All described some form of suicidal thinking, intent, or attempt. Moreover, subjects were represented in levels 2 through 5. Level 2 subjects (suicidal ideation only) considered suicide because of parents who were unsupportive or unemployed, or because friends, boyfriends, or girlfriends were rejecting. Level 3 examples included suicidal threats that resulted from fear of not living up to parents' expectations. For example, one young man kept his father's loaded gun in his closet and talked about shooting himself if he did not make the high school football team. Level 4 examples, involving mild attempts, included students who tried to slit their wrists, or who took pills, typically because of feelings of rejection and hopelessness about the future of their relationships. The one level 5 individual, who had made a serious attempt, described how he drank a combination of household cleaners and medication, for which he received medical attention. His reasons included lack of support and abuse from parents.

Within our normative sample, we also found a very systematic relationship: the more severe the Pfeffer level, the greater the suicidal ideation on our measure (Harter, Marold, and Whitesell, 1992), suggesting both the validity and utility of this self-report measure as a screening instrument. Among our inpatient sample of adolescents with psychiatric diagnoses of depression, we also had data in the charts on Pfeffer's levels. Those who had engaged in serious attempts reported, on our suicidal ideation subscale, more suicidal ideation than did those reporting mild attempts or threats. Of special interest was a subgroup who reported suicidal ideation on our instrument but who were not identified by the clinicians on the unit as potentially suicidal. One of these adolescents, who had two years earlier taken one hundred pills in a suicide attempt but changed her mind and had her stomach pumped, denied any current suicidal thinking in clinical interviews. However, during psychological testing, she was quoted as telling the examiner that "If I were thinking about suicide, I wouldn't tell adults if I was suicidal because I don't trust them, I would only tell my friends." Yet, in the somewhat more impersonal process of taking our self-report instrument, this young woman was able to reveal that she was, indeed, thinking a great deal about suicide. Thus, while we acknowledge the importance of converging methods to obtain information about the dimensions of depression among adolescents, there is considerable evidence that self-report instruments add significantly to our understanding of these dimensions and to the diagnostic process.

General Models Versus Identification of Subgroups of Adolescents at Risk

Most recently, we have found that the general model does not apply equally well to all individuals in that there are different pathways with regard to the sources of self-esteem. There are also differences in the pattern of scores across the dimensions of depression.

Individual Differences in Sources of Self-Esteem. In our previous modeling efforts (Harter, 1986, 1990), we interpreted our findings as evidence for the additive effects of competence or adequacy (derived from James) and social support (derived from Cooley) on self-esteem, each contributing relatively equally. However, in examining patterns of scores for individuals, we discovered clear differences in the particular sources on which adolescents based their self-esteem (Harter, Simon, and Johnson, 1992). For 50 percent of the sample, the additive model applied in that competence or adequacy in domains of importance as well as social support from sources of importance proved highly predictive of self-esteem. However, there was also a subgroup who operated primarily according to the model of the looking glass self in that the primary source of self-esteem was the approval of significant others. Finally, there was a subgroup who based their self-esteem primarily on competence or adequacy, in contrast to support.

For individuals, it is critical to identify their particular sources of low self-esteem. One should not assume that the general additive model necessarily applies to all troubled youth. For example, one fourteen-year-old diabetic female in our clinical sample was admitted to the psychiatric inpatient unit due to increased depression, failure to follow her diet to control her diabetes, and prolonged truancy from school. On our measures, she reported the lowest possible self-esteem, as well as depressed affect and hopelessness. She viewed herself as totally inadequate in the domains of appearance, scholastic competence, and athletic competence and was also quite hopeless, particularly in the domain of appearance. In contrast to this very bleak pattern for competence and adequacy, this young woman reported that she was receiving adequate support from her parents and even more support from peers. Thus, the primary source of her low self-esteem involved her sense of inadequacy, particularly her feelings of unattractiveness, and not lack of support.

Her profile, therefore, clearly pinpointed specific areas for intervention. When her profile was shared with the unit staff, they were surprised, since they perceived this young woman as "cute, vivacious, and attractive." The client acknowledged that "people tell me I'm cute, but I look in the mirror, and don't believe them." Subsequent to our testing, the unit staff began to focus more on her concerns about her unattractiveness, which were primarily based on the scarring caused by multiple intramuscular injections. This, in turn, led to a plan to use an insulin pump to prevent further scarring, as well as surgery to correct the abdominal scarring that had already occurred.

Unlike this young woman, other adolescents, in both our normative and clinical samples, reported that the primary sources of their low self-esteem and depression involved lack of support from either parents or peers. For still others, low self-esteem was based on both feelings of inadequacy as well as lack of support. The value of our profiles, however, even in these latter cases where the additive model applied, is the identification of the *particular* domains or sources of support that put the individual at risk.

Individual Differences in Profiles Across the Dimensions of Depression. Just as there are differences in the patterns of scores that define the antecedents of these depressive reactions, so too there are individual differences in the patterns of scores that define depressive reactions, and differences in the profiles of scores that represent the dimensions of depression. In developing our Dimensions of Depression Profile (Harter, Nowakowski, and Marold,

1989), we identified six different dimensions, each of which is assessed by a separate subscale: (1) affect (cheerful to depressed), (2) self-esteem, (3) hopelessness, (4) energy level, (5) suicidal ideation, and (6) self-blame. This approach is to be contrasted to measurement strategies that involve a single-score approach. However, a dimensional approach will only have merit if it can be demonstrated that there are meaningful patterns of scores across the dimensions that relate to risk.

Thus, we sought to identify patterns among just those middle-school and high school students who reported the most cardinal symptom of depression, depressed affect, since they would appear to be potentially at risk. Five patterns captured the profiles of those adolescents. Recall that low scores represent more negative outcomes, such as depressed mood, low self-esteem, hopelessness, low energy, the presence of self-blame, and the presence of suicidal ideation. In Profile A, all six scores on the depression composite were low. Thus, in addition to being affectively depressed, this group reported low self-esteem, hopelessness, low energy level, suicidal ideation, and self-blame. In Profile B, all scores were low except energy. Thus, although these individuals reported depressed affect, low self-esteem, hopelessness, suicidal ideation, and self-blame, their energy level was reasonably high (with implications that we explore below). In Profile C, all scores were low except suicidal ideation. Thus, although these individuals felt affectively depressed, with little esteem for the self, were hopeless, had low energy, and blamed the self, they did not report suicidal thinking. In Profile D, all scores were high except depressed affect. Thus, although affectively depressed, these individuals did not report the characteristically low self-esteem, nor did they feel hopeless, have low energy, or report suicidal thinking. In Profile E, all scores were high except suicidal ideation. This was the only subgroup that did not report depressed affect but was included given the prevalence of suicidal thinking.

Interviews with a subsample of individuals shed further light on the potential dynamics within certain profiles. We are speculating that those displaying Profile B, reporting depressed affect, low self-esteem, hopelessness, self-blame, and suicidal ideation in consort with high energy, may be most at risk for suicide. More adolescents in this group had made actual attempts, which require some mobilization of energy. Those displaying Profile D, reporting depressed affect, are of particular interest given that they do not conform to the general finding that mood, self-esteem, and hopelessness are highly correlated. Comments from the interviews suggest that these adolescents may have been experiencing a reactive depression to a loss, which did not take its toll on self-esteem. Those displaying Profile E are noteworthy given the prevalence of suicidal thinking in the absence of any other depressive symptoms. Interview material revealed that many of these adolescents were thinking more hypothetically about suicide, often because a friend or family member had made an attempt. However, they did not appear at risk for a suicidal gesture.

As noted above, it may be the case that the second pattern, where an adolescent reports depressed mood, low self-esteem, hopelessness, self-blame, and suicidal ideation but relatively high energy, puts one at the greatest risk for a suicidal attempt. One adolescent male, who first appeared in our normative high school sample and was subsequently hospitalized on the psychiatric unit where we conducted our research, provides a case example. At the time of his first testing, this young man reported depressed affect, low self-esteem, hopelessness, self-blame, suicidal thinking, but moderately high energy. His overall pattern of scores is of special interest given that the psychosocial factors putting him most at risk involved his reported lack of support from both parents as well as peers (rather than adequacy). He was particularly hopeless about obtaining his parents' support, which he also perceived as exceedingly conditional, leading him to extreme forms of false-self behavior.

In an interview, he shared his hopelessness about ever pleasing his parents. His primary area of interest was dirt-bike riding, where he had won several competitions. However, his parents did not approve of this particular sport and were threatening to take his bike away, in part because of his low grades. His parents also expressed their disapproval over his appearance, notably his long hair and his clothing. He described his parents, both professionals, as busy people who were demanding and emotionally unavailable. What support he did receive was described as very conditional. Because his father was in the military, the family moved frequently, thus making it difficult for him to break in to school cliques. As a result, he described his peer support as conditional on behaving in ways that were acceptable to classmates. At the time of the first testing, his primary source of support was a new girlfriend.

With regard to suicidal behavior, he told us that "I sure think a lot about killing myself if this life doesn't get much better." He described what he called "chicken" behaviors, where he would light matches and place them under his nails to see how long he could tolerate the pain. He also related an incident in which he drove his dirt bike toward the edge of a cliff but then spun out just before going over. Shortly thereafter, he had a serious one-car accident, precipitated by his girlfriend's sudden breakup with him. Events surrounding this accident, as well as the threat of suspension from school because of an incident in which he was caught drinking at a high school function, prompted his admission into the psychiatric unit. This youth was on a course that may have led to even more serious suicidal attempts, had he not been hospitalized. From the descriptive material, it is clear that he had the energy to engage in behaviors that put his life in danger. Thus, his profile, with low scores on all dimensions except energy, was illuminating in its potential for identifying adolescents who may be particularly at risk for suicidal behaviors.

In general, our findings suggest the fruitfulness of examining profiles across the dimensions of depression, rather than employing single-score approaches. The potential for risk may well relate to the particular pattern of scores across the dimensions of depression, although there is considerable work to be done to document these links. In addition to these profiles, our analysis of the relative contribution of competence or adequacy concerns versus difficulties in obtaining needed support from significant others also revealed that there are different pathways to depression. Thus, although our general model clearly identifies a number of risk factors that are highly predictive of the depression composite and suicidal ideation, we view it as a backdrop against which we can identify the particular predisposing conditions present for a given adolescent. Toward this goal, we feel that our self-report instruments are particularly useful for pinpointing potential risk factors that can then serve as the basis for intervention.

References

Abramson, L. Y., Seligman, M.E.P., and Teasedale, J. D. "Learned Helplessness in Humans: Critique and Reformulation." In J. C. Coyne (ed.), *Essential Papers on Depression*. New York: New York University Press, 1986.

Alcohol, Drug Abuse, and Mental Health Administration. *Report of the Secretary's Task Force on Youth Suicide*. DHHS Publication No. ADM 89-1621. Washington, D.C.: Government Printing Office, 1989.

Asarnow, J., Carlson, G., and Guthrie, D. "Coping Strategies, Self-Perceptions, Hopelessness, and Perceived Family Environments in Depressed and Suicidal Children." *Journal of Consulting and Clinical Psychology*, 1987, 55, 361–366.

Barrera, M. "Models of Social Support and Life Stress: Beyond the Buffering Hypothesis." In L. H. Cohen (ed.), *Life Events and Psychological Functioning: Theoretical and Methodological Issues*. Newbury Park, Calif.: Sage, 1988.

Baumeister, R. F. "Suicide as Escape from Self." *Psychological Review*, 1990, 97, 90–113.

Beck, A. T. *Depression: Causes and Treatments*. Philadelphia: University of Pennsylvania Press, 1975.

Beck, A. T., Kovacs, M., and Weissman, A. "Hopelessness and Suicidal Behavior." *Journal of the American Medical Association* 1975, 8, 29–38.

Berman, A. L. "Child and Adolescent Suicide: From the Nomothetic to the Idiographic." In A. A. Leenaars (ed.), *Life Span Perspectives of Suicide*. New York: Plenum, 1991.

Bibring, E. "The Mechanism of Depression." In P. Greenacre (ed.), *Affective Disorders: Psychoanalytic Contribution to Their Study*. Madison, Conn.: International Universities Press, 1953.

Blatt, S. J. "Levels of Object Representation in Anaclitic and Introjective Depression." *Psychoanalytic Study of the Child*, 1974, 29, 107–157.

Bleiberg, E. "Narcissistic Disorders in Children." *Bulletin of the Menninger Clinic*, 1984, 48, 501–517.

Bonner, R. L., and Rich, A. R. "Toward a Predictive Model of Suicidal Ideation and Behavior: Some Preliminary Data in College Students." *Suicide and Life-Threatening Behavior*, 1987, 17 (1), 50–63.

Broughton, J. "The Divided Self in Adolescence." *Human Development*, 1981, 24, 13–32.

Brown, B. "Peer Groups and Peer Cultures." In S. S. Feldman and G. R. Elliot (eds.), *At the Threshold: The Developing Adolescent*. Cambridge, Mass.: Harvard University Press, 1990.

Cantor, P. "Young People in Crisis: How You Can Help." Film, National Committee on Youth Suicide Prevention and American Association of Suicidology, in consultation with Harvard Medical School, Department of Psychiatry, Cambridge Hospital, 1987.

Carlson, G. A., and Cantwell, D. P. "Suicidal Behavior and Depression in Children and Adolescents." *Journal of the American Academy of Child and Adolescent Psychiatry*, 1982, 21, 361–368.

Carlson, G. A., and Garber, J. "Developmental Issues in the Classification of Depression in Children." In M. Rutter, C. E. Izard, and P. B. Read (eds.), *Depression in Young People: Developmental and Clinical Perspectives.* New York: Guilford, 1986.

Cicchetti, D., and Schneider-Rosen, K. "An Organizational Approach to Childhood Depression." In M. Rutter, C. E. Izard, and P. B. Read (eds.), *Depression in Young People: Developmental and Clinical Perspectives.* New York: Guilford, 1986.

Cohen, S., and Wills, T. A. "Stress, Social Support, and the Buffering Hypothesis." *Psychological Bulletin,* 1985, *98* (2), 310–357.

Cooley, C. H. *Human Nature and the Social Order.* New York: Charles Scribner's Sons, 1902.

Cooper, C. R., Grotevant, H. D., and Condon, S. M. "Individuality and Connectedness: Both Father and Adolescent Identity Formation and Role-Taking Skills." In H. D. Grotevant and C. R. Cooper (eds.), *Adolescent Development in the Family.* New Directions for Child Development, no. 22. San Francisco: Jossey-Bass, 1983.

Cummings, E. M., and Cicchetti, D. "Toward a Transactional Model of Relations Between Attachment and Depression." In M. T. Greenberg, D. Cicchetti, and E. M. Cummings (eds.), *Attachment in the Preschool Years.* Chicago: University of Chicago Press, 1990.

Deci, E. L., and Ryan, R. M. *Intrinsic Motivation and Self-Determination in Human Behavior.* New York: Plenum, 1985.

Eisenberg, L. "Adolescent Suicide: On Taking Arms Against a Sea of Troubles." *Pediatrics,* 1980, *66,* 315–320.

Emery, P. E. "Adolescent Depression and Suicide." *Adolescence, 1983, 11,*245-258.

Freud, S. "Mourning and Melancholia." In J. Strachey (ed.), *The Standard Edition of the Complete Works of Sigmund Freud.* Vol. 14. London: Hogarth Press, 1968. (Originally published 1917.)

Furman, W. "The Development of Children's Social Networks." In D. Belle (ed.), *Children's Social Networks and Social Supports.* New York: Wiley, 1989.

Garmezy, N., and Rutter, M. (eds.). *Stress, Coping, and Development in Children.* New York: Donnelley and Sons, 1985.

Garrison, C. Z. "The Study of Suicidal Behavior in the Schools." *Suicide and Life-Threatening Behavior,* 1989, *19,* 120–130.

Goldney, R. D. "Parental Representation in Young Women Who Attempt Suicide." *Acta Psychiatry Scandinavia,* 1985, *72,* 230–232.

Gotlib, I. H., and Hammen, C. *Psychological Aspects of Depression: Toward a Cognitive Interpersonal Integration.* New York: Guilford, 1993.

Grotevant, H. D., and Cooper, C. R. "Individuation in Family Relationships." *Human Development,* 1986, *29,* 83–100.

Hammen, C. "Cognitive, Life Stress, and Interpersonal Approaches to a Developmental Psychopathology Model of Depression." *Development and Psychopathology,* 1992, *4,* 189–206.

Hammen, C., and Goodman-Brown, T. "Self-Schemas and Vulnerability to Specific Life Stress in Children at Risk for Depression." *Cognitive Therapy and Research,* 1990, *14,* 215–227.

Harter, S. "Processes Underlying the Construction, Maintenance, and Enhancement of the Self-Concept in Children." In J. Suls and A. G. Greenwald (eds.), *Psychological Perspectives on the Self.* Vol. 3. Hillsdale, N.J.: Erlbaum, 1986.

Harter, S. "Self and Identity Development." In S. S. Feldman and G. R. Elliot (eds.), *At the Threshold: The Developing Adolescent.* Cambridge, Mass.: Harvard University Press, 1990.

Harter, S., Marold, D. B., and Jackson, B. "The Directionality of the Link Between Self-Esteem and Depressed Affect as Experienced by Adolescents." Paper presented at the biennial meeting of the Society for Research in Child Development, Seattle, Apr. 1991.

Harter, S., Marold, D. B., and Whitesell, N. R. "A Model of Psychosocial Risk Factors Leading to Suicidal Ideation in Young Adolescents." *Development and Psychopathology,* 1992, *4,* 167–188.

Harter, S., Nowakowski, M., and Marold, D. B. *The Dimensions of Depression Profile for Children and Adolescents: Revision.* Denver: University of Denver, 1989.

Harter, S., Simon, V. A., and Johnson, E. A. "Common Profiles Across the Dimensions of Depression for Adolescents Who May Be at Risk." Unpublished manuscript, University of Denver, 1992.

Hawton, K. Suicide and Attempted Suicide Among Children and Adolescents. Newbury Park, Calif.: Sage, 1986.

Hawton, K., Cole, D., and O'Grady, M. "Motivational Aspects of Deliberate Self-Poisoning in Adolescents." British Journal of Psychiatry, 1982, 141, 286–291.

Jacobs, J. Adolescent Suicide. New York: Wiley-Interscience, 1971.

James, W. Psychology: The Briefer Course. Troy, Mo.: Holt, Rinehart & Winston, 1892.

Kaslow, N. J., Rehm, L. P., and Siegel, A. W. "Social-Cognitive and Cognitive Correlates of Depression in Children." Journal of Abnormal Child Psychology, 1984, 12, 605–620.

Kazdin, A. E. "Assessment Techniques for Childhood Depression: A Critical Appraisal." Journal of the American Academy of Child and Adolescent Psychiatry, 1981, 20, 358–375.

Kazdin, A. E. "Applications of Self-Report Measures with Children and Adolescents." In A. M. La Greca (ed.), Childhood Assessment: Through the Eyes of the Child. Needham Heights, Mass.: Allyn & Bacon, 1990.

Kendall, P. C., Cantwell, D. P., and Kazdin, A. E. "Depression in Children and Adolescents: Assessment Issues and Recommendations." Cognitive Therapy and Research, 1989, 13, 109–146.

Kovacs, M., and Beck, A. T. "An Empirical-Clinical Approach Towards a Definition of Childhood Depression." In J. G. Schulterbrandt and A. Raskin (eds.), Depression in Childhood: Diagnosis, Treatment, and Conceptual Models. New York: Raven Press, 1977.

Kovacs, M., and Beck, A. T. "Maladaptive Cognitive Structures in Depression." In J. C. Coyne (ed.), Essential Papers on Depression. New York: New York University Press, 1986.

La Greca, A. M. (ed.). Childhood Assessment: Through the Eyes of the Child. Needham Heights, Mass.: Allyn & Bacon, 1990.

McCauley, E., Mitchell, J. R., Burke, P., and Moss, S. "Cognitive Attributes of Depression in Children and Adolescents." Journal of Consulting and Clinical Psychology, 1988, 56, 903–908.

McIntosh, J. L. "Epidemiology of Suicide in the United States." In A. A. Leenaars (ed.), Life Span Perspectives of Suicide. New York: Plenum, 1991.

Maris, R. W. "The Developmental Perspective of Suicide." In A. A. Leenaars (ed.), Life Span Perspectives of Suicide. New York: Plenum, 1991.

Marold, D. B. "Correlates of Suicidal Ideation Among Young Adolescents." Unpublished doctoral dissertation, University of Denver, 1987.

Motto, J. A. "Suicide in Male Adolescents." In H. S. Sudak, A. B. Ford, and N. B. Rushforth (eds.), Suicide in the Young. Boston: Wright, 1984.

Myers, K., Burke, P., and McCauley, E. "Suicidal Behavior by Hospitalized Preadolescent Children in a Psychiatric Unit." Journal of the American Academy of Child and Adolescent Psychiatry, 1985, 24, 474–480.

Nolen-Hoeksema, S., Girgus, J. S., and Seligman, M.E.P. "Learned Helplessness in Children: A Longitudinal Study of Depression, Achievement, and Explanatory Style." Journal of Personality and Social Psychology, 1986, 51, 435–442.

Pfeffer, C. R. The Suicidal Child. New York: Guilford, 1986.

Pfeffer, C. R. "Risk Factors Associated with Youth Suicide: A Clinical Perspective." Psychiatric Annals, 1988, 18, 652–656.

Pfeffer, C. R. "Life Stress and Family Risk Factors for Youth Fatal and Nonfatal Suicidal Behavior." In C. R. Pfeffer (ed.), Suicide Among Youth: Perspectives on Risk and Prevention. Washington, D.C.: American Psychiatric Press, 1989.

Pfeffer, C., Lipkins, M. A., Plutchik, R., and Mizruchi, M. "Normal Children at Risk for Suicidal Behavior: A Two-Year Follow-Up Study." Journal of the American Academy of Child and Adolescent Psychiatry, 1988, 27, 34–41.

Pfeffer, C. R., Newcorn, J., and Kaplan, G. "Suicidal Behavior in Adolescent Psychiatric Inpatients." Journal of the American Academy of Child and Adolescent Psychiatry, 1988, 27, 357–361.

Pfeffer, C. R., Plutchik, R., and Mizruchi, M. "Suicidal and Assaultive Behavior in Children: Classification, Measurement, and Interrelations." *American Journal of Psychiatry,* 1983, *14,* 154–157.

Plutchik, R., and Conte, H. "Self-Report Scales for the Measurement of Depression." *Psychiatric Annals,* 1989, *19* (7), 367–371.

Pyszcynski, T., and Greenberg, J. "Self-Regulatory Perseveration and the Depressive Self-Focusing Style: A Self-Awareness Theory of Reactive Depression." *Psychological Bulletin,* 1987, *102,* 122–138.

Renouf, A. G., and Harter, S. "Low Self-Worth and Anger as Components of the Depressive Experience in Young Adolescents." *Development and Psychopathology,* 1990, *2,* 293–310.

Rogers, C., and Dymond, R. *Psychotherapy and Personality Change.* Chicago: University of Chicago Press, 1954.

Rosenberg, M. *Conceiving the Self.* New York: Basic Books, 1979.

Rosenberg, M. "Self-Concept from Middle Childhood Through Adolescence." In J. Suls and A. G. Greenwald (eds.), *Psychological Perspectives on the Self.* Vol. 3. Hillsdale, N.J.: Erlbaum, 1986.

Rudd, M. D. "The Prevalence of Suicidal Ideation Among College Students." *Suicide and Life-Threatening Behavior,* 1989, *19,* 173–183.

Rutter, M. "Psychosocial Resilience and Protective Mechanisms." *American Journal of Orthopsychiatry,* 1987, *57,* 47–61.

Rutter, M. "Epidemiological Approaches to Developmental Psychopathology." *Archives of General Psychiatry,* 1988, *45,* 486–495.

Rutter, M. "Isle of Wight Revisited: Twenty-Five Years of Child Psychiatric Epidemiology." *Journal of the American Academy of Child and Adolescent Psychiatry,* 1989, *28,* 633–653.

Rutter, M., Izard, C. E., and Read, P. B. (eds.). *Depression in Childhood: Developmental Perspectives.* New York: Guilford, 1985.

Sandler, I. N., Miller, P., Short, J., and Wolchik, S. A. In D. Belle (ed.), *Children's Social Networks and Social Supports.* New York: Wiley, 1989.

Savin-Williams, R. C., and Berndt, T. "Friendship During Adolescence." In S. S. Feldman and G. R. Elliot (eds.), *At the Threshold: The Developing Adolescent.* Cambridge, Mass.: Harvard University Press, 1990.

Schneidman, E. S. "The Commonalities of Suicide Across the Life Span." In A. A. Leenaars (ed.), *Life Span Perspectives of Suicide.* New York: Plenum, 1991.

Seligman, M.E.P. *Helplessness: On Depression, Development, and Death.* New York: W. H. Freeman, 1975.

Selman, R. *The Growth of Interpersonal Understanding.* San Diego: Academic Press, 1980.

Shaffer, D. "Depression and Suicide in Children and Adolescents." In M. Rutter and L. Hersov (eds.), *Child and Adolescent Psychiatry: Modern Approaches.* (2nd ed.) Oxford, England: Blackwell, 1985.

Smith, K., and Crawford, S. "Suicidal Behavior Among Normal High School Students." *Suicide and Life-Threatening Behavior,* 1986, *16,* 313–325.

Spirato, A., Brown, L., Overholser, J., and Fritz, G. "Attempted Suicide in Adolescence: A Review and Critique of the Literature." *Clinical Psychology Review,* 1989, *9,* 335–363.

Sroufe, L. A. "Infant-Caregiver Attachment and Patterns of Adaptation in the Preschool: The Roots of Competence and Maladaption." In M. Perlmutter (ed.), *Minnesota Symposia in Child Psychology.* Vol. 16. Hillsdale, N.J.: Erlbaum, 1983.

Sroufe, L. A., and Rutter, M. "The Domain of Developmental Psychopathology." *Child Development,* 1985, *55,* 17–29.

Steinberg, L. "Autonomy, Conflict, and Harmony in the Family." In S. S. Feldman and G. R. Elliot (eds.), *At the Threshold: The Developing Adolescent.* Cambridge, Mass.: Harvard University Press, 1990.

Topol, P., and Reznikoff, M. "Perceived Peer and Family Relationships, Hopelessness, and Locus of Control as Factors in Adolescent Suicide Attempts." *Suicide and Life-Threatening Behavior,* 1982, *12,* 141–150.

Velez, C. N., and Cohen, P. "Suicidal Behavior and Ideation in a Community Sample of Children: Maternal and Youth Report." *Journal of the American Academy of Child and Adolescent Psychiatry*, 1988, 27, 349–356.

Winnicott, D. *The Maturational Processes and the Facilitating Environment.* Madison, Conn.: International Universities Press, 1965.

SUSAN HARTER is professor of psychology and developmental psychology area head at the University of Denver.

DONNA B. MAROLD is a research associate at the University of Denver as well as a licensed psychologist and marriage and family therapist in private practice.

Depression rates, IQ, knowledge of the finality of death, exposure to suicidal behavior, and knowledge of suicidal methods differed between suicidal and nonsuicidal psychiatrically hospitalized children and developmentally delayed adolescents and had different impacts depending on age and development.

Developmental Aspects of Suicidal Behavior in Children and Developmentally Delayed Adolescents

Gabrielle A. Carlson, Joan R. Asarnow, Israel Orbach

The rapid rise in suicidal behavior in young people in recent years has brought a profusion of studies and theories attempting to explain the statistics and stem the tide of such behavior. Suicide rates begin to rise rapidly with adolescence, which suggests that younger children are relatively protected and that, subsequently, biological maturity, cognitive maturity, and experience and exposure somehow combine to erode that protection (Hollinger and Offer, 1989; Shaffer and Fisher, 1981). Although mental illness in general and depressive disorders in particular are very commonly found in people who kill themselves, there is some indication that age has an impact on the particular diagnoses that prevail. In general, whereas major depressive disorders are more common in middle-age and older people, a mixed diagnostic picture (that is, mood disorder comorbid with substance abuse or conduct disorder) occurs in the younger population (Carlson, Asarnow, and Orbach, 1987; Rich, Young, and Fowler, 1986).

The question of what accounts for relatively few suicides in youngsters before age fifteen has not been answered. In an earlier study (Carlson, Asarnow, and Orbach, 1987), we examined knowledge and attitudes about suicide in psychiatrically hospitalized children and developmentally delayed adolescents with mental ages between eight and thirteen and in a nonpsychiatric "normal" control group with a similar age range. We were interested in what mental illness conferred on such knowledge and attitudes, whether these changed with age through late childhood, and, insofar as was possible, whether changes that occurred at adolescence had to do with chronological age or mental age. Using a semistructured interview about death and suicide, we found that younger suicidal children and below-grade-level children were, in fact, less interested in and knowledgeable about suicide *regardless* of their psychiatric status. Knowledge of the irreversibility of death was not completely accepted until adolescence. When asked about possible means of suicide, regardless of their psychiatric status, eight- to thirteen-year-old children selected more violent (shooting and stabbing) but less accessible means as possible ways in which one might kill himself or herself. In contrast, developmentally delayed adolescents named overdosing and wrist cutting as well as shooting and stabbing as possible means. The biggest difference between children and adolescents involved the consistency among what they thought was lethal, what they thought about doing when they felt suicidal, and what they actually attempted. Among the preadolescents, there was little correspondence; attempts agreed with knowledge or ideation only 20.7 percent of the time. Among adolescents, attempts agreed with knowledge 46.6 percent of the time and with ideation 100 percent of the time ($p < .03$).

We concluded that preadolescent children may seem more knowledgeable about death and suicide than they actually are. The fact that they chose shooting and stabbing as suicide methods probably comes more from interpolating how people kill each other than how one might kill oneself. Adolescents, on the other hand, in spite of the fact that they were functioning academically and psychosocially two to three years younger than their age (M age 14.5 years), seemed more committed to the subject and named the more common, if less lethal, means of overdosing and wrist slashing.

In light of those findings, we decided to explore further whether suicidal children and adolescents differed from their nonsuicidal counterparts with regard to knowledge of death and suicide. We hypothesized that suicidal children and adolescents would be more equivocal about the irreversibility of death, would have more personal acquaintance with suicide, and would have clearer notions about how to commit suicide. Furthermore, findings in our earlier study led us to believe that the older suicidal children would behave more like adolescents in terms of their knowledge about suicide methods. We speculated that younger nonsuicidal children would think that a person who attempts suicide does not really want to die, and that older suicidal youngsters would think the opposite. Finally, by virtue of their likelihood of being depressed, we expected all suicidal subjects would name depression or misery as major motivations for suicide.

Methods

Sample. Two groups of children were included in this study of developmental aspects of suicidal behavior. The first group were children between eight years of age and twelve years and eleven months consecutively admitted to the children's inpatient unit at the Neuropsychiatric Institute of the University of California, Los Angeles. They had to have a mental age of at least eight years, as determined by WISC-R testing, to be included in the sample. The second group were young adolescents, ages thirteen to sixteen, admitted to another inpatient unit serving primarily a mentally retarded or developmentally delayed population.

Assessment of Knowledge of Death and Suicide. Within the first two weeks of psychiatric hospitalization, the children and adolescents were administered the Depression Self-Rating Scale (DSRS) (Birleson, 1981; Birleson, Hudson, Buchanon, and Wolf, 1987; Asarnow and Carlson, 1985), followed by our death-suicide interview (Carlson, Asarnow, and Orbach, 1987). Subjects were not told that this was a study of suicide but rather that we would be asking them some important but difficult questions. The interview schedule, patterned after Koocher's (1973) interview about death, specifically asks children to respond to the following questions: "How do people die?" "What happens to someone after they die?" "Is it possible to come back to life once you're dead?" In the next part of the interview, questions about suicide are asked in the third person with the idea that children may feel less threatened answering questions about someone else: "Do you know anyone who has tried to kill himself or herself?" "What did that person do?" "What would make someone want to do that?" "How would someone kill himself or herself?" Finally, in addition to these hypothetical questions, the subjects were asked, "When do you think you will die?" "Have you ever thought about killing yourself?" "What did you think about doing?" "Do you think you'll come back to life?" "Have you ever tried to kill yourself?" "What did you do?" Scoring for the death-suicide interview is more fully described elsewhere (Carlson, Asarnow, and Orbach, 1987).

Diagnostic Assessment. Diagnostic aspects of the assessment consisted of the (1) Schedule of Affective Disorders and Schizophrenia for Children (K-SADS-E) (Orvaschel and others, 1982; Chambers and others, 1985) administered by a trained research assistant or ward psychiatrist blind to DSRS and suicide data, (2) Child Behavior Checklist (CBCL) (Achenbach and Edelbrock, 1978, 1979, 1983) completed by parents, and (3) routine multidisciplinary evaluation. In this study, the Wechsler Intelligence Scale for Children (Revised) and a final diagnosis were used in data analysis. The final diagnosis was reached by synthesizing data from the K-SADS-E and longitudinal observations made by the primary therapist and interdisciplinary team after the subjects had been evaluated and treated for what was usually three months. The reliability for Principal Axis I diagnoses was $K = .82$ ($p < .0001$), and for depression versus nondepression, $K = .81$ ($p < .0001$) (Asarnow and Carlson, 1985).

Data Analysis. The division between suicidal versus nonsuicidal groups was made on the basis of responses to the death-suicide interview. Children and adolescents who admitted to having thought about killing themselves (not just having wished they were dead) were considered suicidal. Attempters were those who had actually made an attempt regardless of lethality. To examine developmental impact of age on knowledge and experience with suicide, the population was divided into three age groups: eight to ten years old, eleven to thirteen years old, and adolescent (over thirteen years). Data were analyzed using both analysis of variance for continuous variables and chi-square for nonparametric variables.

Results

A total of sixty-one children and twenty-five adolescents were included in the study. Overall, 44.8 percent of the twenty-nine eight- to ten-year-olds, 50 percent of the thirty-two eleven- to thirteen-year-olds, and 60 percent of the twenty-five developmentally delayed adolescents professed to suicidal ideation (*p* was not significant). Among the children, 20.7 percent of those who thought about suicide had no specific plans. Those with plans thought about stabbing (31 percent), overdosing (17 percent), shooting (6.9 percent), and drowning (13.7 percent). Only 8 percent of adolescents had no plans. The ruminations of those with plans included overdosing (40 percent), wrist cutting (40 percent), and jumping (13.3 percent), with stabbing and hanging having one endorsement each.

Tables 6.1 and 6.2 present demographic and clinical characteristics of the suicidal and nonsuicidal children and adolescents. A series of analyses of variance comparing suicidal and nonsuicidal children and adolescents revealed no significant differences in age, overall level of psychopathology (as measured by CBCL *T*-scores), and socioeconomic status (Duncan, 1977). There were, however, notable IQ differences between suicidal and nonsuicidal subjects. In the case of suicidal children, mean verbal IQ was ten points higher than that of nonsuicidal children. In the case of suicidal developmentally delayed adolescents, performance IQ was over twelve points higher than that of their nonsuicidal counterparts.

Diagnostic Status. As expected, both the suicidal children and the suicidal adolescents were significantly more depressed as measured by the DSRS. Overall, significantly more suicidal subjects met criteria for major depression, dysthymic disorder, or adjustment disorder with depressed mood. Whereas 59

Table 6.1. Demographic Data: Psychiatrically Hospitalized Children

Variable	Suicidal (N = 29)	Nonsuicidal (N = 32)	Significance
Mean age	10.81 ± 0.4	10.34 ± 0.3	ns
Verbal IQ	102 ± 5.6	92.2 ± 15.6	$p < .01$
Performance IQ	106.6 ± 12.4	102.7 ± 16.2	ns
IQ Full-scale	105 ± 8.8	96.8 ± 15.9	$p < .05$
Duncan socioeconomic index	50.3 ± 13.4	61.5 ± 21.2	ns
Mean CBCL *T*-score	75.2 ± 8.8	77.2 ± 7.6	ns
Mean DSRS	14.2 ± 5.7	10.5 ± 4.7	$p < .05$
Mood disorder (%)	.59	.25	$p < .001$
Sex (male:female)	22:7	24:8	ns

Note: CBCL = Child Behavior Checklist; DSRS = Depression Self-Rating Scale; ns = not significant.

Table 6.2. Demographic Data: Developmentally Delayed Adolescents

Variable	Suicidal (N = 15)	Nonsuicidal (N = 10)	Significance
Mean age	14.6 ± 1.5	14.5 ± 1.8	
Verbal IQ	85.7 ±16.3	80.2 ± 13.4	ns
Performance IQ	98.2 ± 18.5	86.0 ± 22.5	$p = .025$
Full-scale IQ	91.0 ± 17.3	81.1 ± 16.5	$p < .05$
Duncan socioeconomic index	46.2 ± 20.1	44.1 ± 30.3	ns
Mean CBCL T-score	75.6 ± 8.3	72.4 ± 8.1	ns
Mean DSRS	16.4 ± 2.6	12.4 ± 4.1	$p = .02$
Mood disorder (%)	.67	0	$p < .001$
Sex (male:female)	4:11	2:10	ns

Note: CBCL = Child Behavior Checklist; DSRS = Depression Self-Rating Scale; ns = not significant.

percent of suicidal children met criteria for mood disorder (major depression, dysthymic disorder, or adjustment disorder with depressed mood), 25 percent of nonsuicidal children met these criteria. In the developmentally delayed adolescents, however, 67 percent of the suicidal group and none of the nonsuicidal group met criteria for mood disorder.

These patterns are further clarified in Table 6.3, which presents the diagnostic distributions of the suicidal and nonsuicidal child and adolescent groups. When we evaluated the distribution of suicidal and nonsuicidal children as a function of subtypes of depression (for example, major depression versus dysthymic disorder), developmental differences emerged. Notably, none of the nonsuicidal adolescents met criteria for either major depression or dysthymic disorder, and suicidal adolescents were significantly more likely than nonsuicidal adolescents to show both of these disorders. On the other hand, among the children, the frequency of major depression was not significantly different in suicidal versus nonsuicidal subjects (24.1 percent versus 15.6 percent, respectively). However, suicidal children were significantly more likely than nonsuicidal children to have dysthymic disorder. Thus, it was the presence of dysthymic disorder that accounted for the difference in depression rates between the suicidal and nonsuicidal children.

Examining the proportion of suicidal and nonsuicidal children within diagnostic groups, we found that significantly more of the subjects with mood disorders were suicidal (76 percent) than were nonsuicidal (24 percent). Children with externalizing behavioral disorders (attention deficit disorder, conduct disorder, and oppositional disorder) were somewhat more likely to be suicidal than those without such disorders, but that did not reach statistical significance. Additionally, because children frequently presented with multiple diagnoses, it is important to note that some of the children with externalizing behavioral disorders also met criteria for depression diagnoses. Suicidal ideation and attempts were uncommon among the few schizophrenic subjects in the study.

**Table 6.3. Percentage Distribution of Subjects
by Diagnosis, Suicidality, and Age**

| Diagnosis | Suicidal | | Nonsuicidal | |
	Children (N = 29)	Adolescents (N = 15)	Children (N = 32)	Adolescents (N = 10)
Major depression	24.1%	46.6%	15.6%	0**
Dysthymia				
and cyclothymia	37.9	40	15.6*	0*
Adjustment disorder	6.8	0	0	0
Conduct and				
oppositional disorders	55.1	0	40.6	30
Attention				
deficit disorder	24.1	13.3	12.5	10
Anxiety disorder	17.3	20	12.5	0
Schizophrenia	0	6.6	9.3	30
Adjustment disorder	6.9	6.6	0	0

Note: Because subjects often met criteria for more than one diagnosis, subjects may be counted in more than one cell of this table.

* $p < .05$ (suicidal versus nonsuicidal children/adolescents)

**$p < .025$ (suicidal versus nonsuicidal children/adolescents)

Death-Suicide Interview. On the death-suicide interview, suicidal subjects showed the same distribution of responses to the question "How do people die?" as that of nonsuicidal subjects. That is, both groups acknowledged natural causes, murder, suicide, or all of them at similar rates. Suicidal youngsters were no more likely to volunteer suicide as a means of death than were nonsuicidal youngsters. Conversely, of those who acknowledged suicide as a means of death, 50 percent admitted to feeling suicidal themselves. With respect to actually knowing someone who had attempted or committed suicide, however, responses between children and adolescents were somewhat different. As indicated in Table 6.4, 87 percent of suicidal adolescents (versus 50 percent of nonsuicidal adolescents) were personally acquainted with someone suicidal ($x^2 = 4.0$, $p = .05$). The difference was not statistically significant in the children.

Two questions produced an interesting interaction between age and suicidal status. To the question "How might someone who wanted to kill himself or herself do it?" the following occurred: Nonsuicidal children and adolescents were most likely to choose violent but less feasible methods such as shooting or stabbing (either as the only means or together with other, less violent but more accessible methods). The youngest suicidal children (ages eight to ten) also picked those methods. Older suicidal children (ages eleven to thirteen) and adolescents were more apt to choose overdose, wrist cutting, running into traffic, drowning, or jumping from buildings, that is, methods that seemed more accessible to them ($p = .02$). These results are summarized in Table 6.5.

Table 6.4. Percentage Distribution of Subjects Reporting Personal Knowledge of a Suicidal Individual, by Age and Suicidal Status

	Children		
Suicidal Status	8–10 years (N = 29)	11–13 years (N = 32)	Adolescents (Older than 13 Years) (N = 25)
Suicidal	69%	75%	87%
Nonsuicidal	44	63	50

Note: Figures are percentages responding yes to the question "Do you know anyone who has tried to kill himself or herself?" Suicidal adolescents were significantly more likely to report personal knowledge of a suicidal individual than were nonsuicidal adolescents.

Somewhat the same age-suicide dichotomy was seen in responses to the question "Would someone who tried to kill himself or herself want to be saved?" As summarized in Table 6.6, older suicidal children and all adolescents were definite about wanting to be saved. Nonsuicidal children, and even the youngest suicidal children, were more equivocal (x^2 = 5.86, p = .05).

Subjects' understanding of the motivation behind suicide did not differ significantly between suicidal and nonsuicidal groups. Younger, nonsuicidal children mostly could not fathom why someone might want to commit suicide. Otherwise, both suicidal and nonsuicidal young people felt that sadness, depression, misery, and self-hatred were somewhat more compelling suicide motives (61 percent) than that of having terrible things happen to oneself (39 percent).

In response to the question "When do you think you will die?" suicidal children and adolescents were just as likely to say they would die of old age as were nonsuicidal subjects. As shown in Table 6.7, the question of whether or not people can come back to life once they are dead was answered similarly by older children and adolescents, regardless of suicidal tendencies. Two-thirds of these subjects recognized that neither they themselves nor anyone else can come back to life once dead (though 27 percent of developmentally delayed adolescents still clung to the notion that their own deaths would not be permanent). On the other hand, among the eight- to ten-year-olds, suicide status may have had an effect. The majority of nonsuicidal youngsters (69 percent) recognized that neither they nor others can come back to life. However, 46 percent of suicidal youngsters felt that they could come back to life. Differences in responses to this question were statistically significant in the eight- to ten-year-old category (x^2 = 6.17, p < .05).

Suicide attempters were also compared with subjects who only thought about suicide. By and large, there were few differences. The attempters were no more depressed than the nonattempters, either diagnostically or by DSRS score. They had no greater psychopathology as measured by the CBCL and

Table 6.5. Percentage Distribution of Subjects Responding to Question on Suicide Method, by Age and Suicide Status

Method	Suicidal Children		Suicidal Adolescents (N = 15)	Nonsuicidal Children		Nonsuicidal Adolescents (N = 10)
	8–10 years (N = 13)	11–13 years (N = 16)		8–10 years (N = 16)	11–13 years (N = 16)	
Shoot, stab	53.8%	18.7%	13.3%	37.5%	50.0%	30.0%
Overdose, run into traffic, drown, jump from building, cut wrists	15.3	43.7	46.6	18.8	18.8	20.0
Both lethal and nonlethal	23.0	37.5	40.0	25.0	31.3	50.0
Don't know	7.7	—	—	18.8	0	0

Note: Figures are percentages responding yes to the question "How might someone who wanted to kill himself or herself do it?"

Table 6.6. Percentage Distribution of Subjects Responding to Question on Wanting to Be Saved from Suicide, by Age and Suicide Status

	Children		
Suicidal Status	8–10 Years (N = 29)	11–13 Years (N = 32)	Adolescents (Older than 13 Years) (N = 25)
Suicidal	54%	75%	67%
Nonsuicidal	47	38	70

Note: Figures are percentages responding yes to the question "Would someone who tried to kill himself or herself want to be saved?" Older suicidal children and all adolescents significantly more frequently thought someone would want to be saved than did all eight- to ten-year-olds and nonsuicidal eleven- to thirteen-year-olds.

were not significantly older, smarter, or less intelligent. On the death-suicide interview, there were only two questions that distinguished the two populations. In justifying why someone might want to commit suicide, attempters were significantly more likely to give external reasons (something terrible happening, no one likes them) than were ideators (56 percent versus 14 percent, respectively; $x^2 = 7.2$, $p = .02$), who felt that unhappiness, anger, or other internal states were more likely motivators. This finding remained valid even when suicide attempters were matched with nonattempters for age, sex, and grade-level status. Finally, attempters were more likely than ideators to say that a person who tried to kill himself or herself would want to be saved (78 percent versus 50 percent, respectively; $x^2 = 5.86$, $p < .05$).

Discussion

As mentioned earlier, our research on children's attitudes toward death and suicide had three goals. The first two, described in an earlier study (Carlson, Asarnow, and Orbach, 1987), were to determine what children between the mental ages of eight and thirteen knew about suicide and death, and to see if their knowledge and attitudes changed with age. The present study examined whether these concepts are influenced by a child's suicidal tendencies.

Relationship to Depression. This study found a closer association in adolescents between depression and suicide than was found in preadolescents. This is, in part, because children could be depressed without being suicidal whereas, in this sample, depressed adolescents were always suicidal. We found previously (Asarnow, Carlson, and Guthrie, 1987; Asarnow and Guthrie, 1989; Carlson and Cantwell, 1982) and others have reported (Kovacs and Puig-Antich, 1989; Pfeffer and others, 1982; Pfeffer, Plutchik, and Mizruchi, 1983; Myers, Burke, and McCauley, 1985; Brent and others, 1986) that depressive disorders in children are neither a necessary nor sufficient cause for suicidal behavior, although, certainly, depression and depressive diagnoses are found with statistically greater frequency among suicidal children and adolescents.

Table 6.7. Percentage Distribution of Subjects Responding to Question on Reversibility of Death, by Age and Suicidal Status

	Suicidal Children		Suicidal Adolescents (N = 15)	Nonsuicidal Children		Nonsuicidal Adolescents (N = 10)
Response	8–10 years (N = 13)	11–13 years (N = 16)		8–10 years (N = 16)	11–13 years (N = 16)	
Neither self nor others can come back to life	31%	69%	67%	69%	56%	80%
Others (but not self) can come back to life	23	19	0	19	19	—
Self (but not others) can come back to life	46	12	33	6	12	20
Both self and others can come back to life	0	0	0	6	12	0

Note: Figures are percentages responding yes to the question "Is it possible to come back to life once you're dead?"

Whether the difference between children and adolescents with regard to this association is idiosyncratic to the population studied, reflects different motivations among children and adolescents, or points out our inability to define depression in less verbal children who do not articulate their feelings and symptoms in recognizable ways remains to be clarified.

Suicidal Ideation Versus Attempt. There were greater differences between suicidal and nonsuicidal youngsters than there were between subjects who thought about suicide and those who attempted. Besides the diagnostic differences, suicidal youngsters had higher IQs. This was true for both the intellectually normal preadolescents, who had significantly higher IQs, and the developmentally delayed adolescents, who had significantly higher performance IQs than those of nonsuicidal subjects. This was not true for attempters. As we have reported previously (Carlson, Asarnow, and Orbach, 1987), interest in suicide was lowest among eight- to ten-year-olds who were below grade level and thus the least mature children. Although we found no change in suicidal ideation with age per se, the rate of suicidal ideation was twice as high among eleven- to thirteen-year-old grade-level children when compared to eight- to ten-year-old below-grade-level children ($p < .01$). We suspect that the higher IQs among suicidal children reflect the association between suicidality and cognitive maturity. On the other hand, as we reported earlier, the rate of suicidal ideation was very similar for eleven- to thirteen-year-old grade-level children (66.6 percent) and the developmentally delayed and below-grade-level adolescents (60 percent). However, suicide attempts more than doubled (22.2 percent for eleven- to thirteen-year-olds versus 48 percent for adolescents), suggesting that more than cognitive maturity is operating in the progression from ideation to suicide attempt. The literature is mixed regarding the consistency with which higher IQ is associated with suicidal behavior. Shaffer (1974) found that his twelve- to fourteen-year-olds who eventually completed suicide had higher IQs. The Terman study (Schneidman, 1976) following gifted children into adulthood found a significantly higher suicide rate compared to the "normal" population. Myers, Burke, and McCauley (1985) noted a similar finding in a hospitalized sample of suicidal youngsters, although several other studies did not (Asarnow and Guthrie, 1989; Weiner and Pfeffer, 1987). Despite the need to further clarify this finding, it is possible that higher IQ makes two contributions to suicide risk. First, in younger children, higher IQ may lead to an increased awareness of suicide. Second, increasing age confers a greater ability to plan and execute a successful suicide.

The differences in responses to the death-suicide questions between suicidal and nonsuicidal subjects may shed some light on what factors do and do not contribute to suicidal behavior. Although we expected suicidal children to be more preoccupied with suicide and therefore to suggest it more often as a response to the question "How do people die?" this was not the case. This means that children who admit to thinking about suicide at certain times are not always thinking about it, and that nonsuicidal children are equally aware of it as a means of death. On the other hand, significantly more suicidal subjects admitted that they knew of someone who had attempted or committed suicide. This was particularly significant among adolescents. Thus, closer contact with suicidal people may have more impact on suicidal behavior than does the abstract knowledge that suicide is a means of death. Furthermore, this knowledge may be more compelling in vulnerable adolescents. There are reports (Gould and Shaffer, 1986; Phillips and Carstensen, 1986) suggesting a modeling component to suicidal behavior, especially among adolescents.

A question of great interest to us was whether children's suicide attempts were unsuccessful because they did not know how to commit suicide or were simply unable to access the means. The responses we obtained mirrored what we reported earlier just by looking at changes with age, grade level, and psychiatric status. It appeared that children know about violent death but not necessarily about suicide. The fact that the younger nonsuicidal eleven- to thirteen-year-olds more often suggested such lethal means as shooting and stabbing, whereas suicidal older children and all adolescents suggested the more typical, accessible means, was the seeming paradox. However, we concluded that while the former group seemed knowledgeable, in fact, more knowledgeable than their suicidal counterparts, they were not so much thinking about suicide as they were simply assuming that one kills oneself the same way in which one kills anyone else—by shooting or stabbing. This was the most sensible explanation we could find to justify the preoccupation children have with stabbing, a fairly uncommon means of suicide in the United States, and the observation that so many children threaten to kill themselves with a kitchen knife.

Although we had predicted the former observation, a seeming paradox occurred in answer to the question "Would someone who tried to kill himself or herself want to be saved?" We had hypothesized that younger children and nonsuicidal children, frightened by the thought of dying and appalled by the thought of self-destruction, would readily agree that no one really wants to die. Conversely, we hypothesized that those who had considered suicide as the solution to their anguish would expect that suicidal others do not want to be saved. The fact that this did not occur may mean that nonsuicidal (lower IQ) and younger children are more concrete and figure that if someone makes an attempt, they want to be dead. Similarly, older and suicidal youngsters recognized a certain amount of ambivalence in suicidal behavior. The fact that significantly more attempters than ideators (78 percent versus 50 percent, respectively) reported that someone making an attempt would want to be saved also suggests that they recognized an attempt may mean more than an effort to die and be done with life.

It has been suggested that one of the factors that protects children from suicide is their fluid concept of the reversibility of death. As we reported earlier (Carlson, Asarnow, and Orbach, 1987), our findings confirm those of others in that, with age, more subjects are convinced about the permanence of death. In examining this hypothesis with suicidal youngsters, there again appeared to be a spectrum of responses. While the majority of children and adolescents (57 to 80 percent) felt that no one could come back to life once dead, the majority of the youngest suicidal children felt that not only could "people" come back to life (23 percent) but *they* could come back to life (46 percent). It is difficult to understand how this is protective, but it does underscore that although children seem knowledgeable about death and suicide, their comprehension is incomplete and tenuous.

Carlson and Cantwell (1982) reported that suicide attempters are not necessarily on a continuum with suicidal ideators. Although other studies have concluded differently (for example, Brent and others, 1986), the data from this undertaking again do not suggest that suicide attempters are simply more extreme versions of suicide ideators. Attempters were not older, smarter, more depressed, or better informed about suicide than were ideators. Except for stating more often that attempters would want to be saved, the only other difference on the death-suicide interview was their responses to the question "Why might someone want to commit suicide?" Suicide ideators, nonsuicidal subjects, and even nonpsychiatric subjects (Carlson, Asarnow, and Orbach, 1987) more frequently endorsed internal states (misery, depression, hopelessness) as motivators. On the other hand, attempters significantly more often justified "someone's" attempt with external events. If this reflects their own motivation to use self-harm when things happen that they do not like, it suggests that poor problem solving rather than internal distress explains why some ideators make an attempt and others do not. This is consistent with other findings indicating that suicidal children and adults show defects in their problem-solving and coping skills (Asarnow, Carlson, and Guthrie, 1987; Schotte and Clum, 1987).

We have reported elsewhere (Asarnow, Carlson, and Guthrie, 1987; Asarnow, 1991) that children who attempt suicide, when compared to nonattempters, are more likely to perceive their family environments as lacking in support and high in conflict. This finding is also consistent with the notion that suicide attempts often represent a breakdown in children's abilities to cope with environmental stress.

Conclusion

In summary, some of our hypotheses were confirmed. Knowledge of the finality of death, exposure to suicide or suicidal behavior, and knowledge of suicide methods differed between suicidal and nonsuicidal children. The most interesting finding, however, was that the variables studied impacted differently depending on age and development (for example, uncertainty about death was important only in the youngest suicidal children, and acquaintance with suicidal behavior had more significance in suicidal adolescents). It is likely, then, that whatever complex interactions are ultimately found to account for suicide in one age group will not necessarily be applicable to another.

References

Achenbach, T. M., and Edelbrock, C. S. "The Classification of Child Psychopathology." *Psychological Bulletin*, 1978, *85*, 1275–1300.

Achenbach, T. M., and Edelbrock, C. S. "The Child Behavior Profile, Part 2: Boys Aged 12–16 and Girls Aged 6–11 and 12–16." *Journal of Consulting and Clinical Psychology*, 1979, *47*, 223–233.

Achenbach, T. M., and Edelbrock, C. S. *Manual for the Child Behavior Checklist and Revised Child Behavior Profile.* Burlington: University of Vermont, 1983.

Asarnow, J. R. "Suicidal Ideation and Attempts During Middle Childhood: Associations with Perceived Family Stress and Depression Among Child Psychiatric Inpatients." *Journal of Clinical Child Psychology*, 1991, *21*, 35–40.

Asarnow, J. R., and Carlson, G. A. "The Depression Self-Rating Scale: Utility with Child Psychiatric Inpatients." *Journal of Consulting and Clinical Psychology*, 1985, *53*,491–499.

Asarnow, J. R., Carlson, G. A., and Guthrie, D. "Coping Strategies, Self-Perceptions, Hopelessness, and Perceived Family Environments in Depressed and Suicidal Children." *Journal of Consulting and Clinical Psychology*, 1987, *55*, 361–366.

Asarnow, J. R., and Guthrie, D. "Suicidal Behavior, Depression, and Hopelessness in Child Psychiatric Inpatients: A Replication and Extension." *Journal of Clinical Child Psychology*, 1989, *18*, 129–136.

Birleson, P. "The Validity of Depressive Disorders and the Development of a Self-Rating Scale: A Research Report." *Journal of Child Psychology and Psychiatry and Allied Disciplines*, 1981, *22*, 73–86.

Birleson, P., Hudson, I., Buchanon, G., and Wolf, S. "Clinical Evaluation of a Self-Rating Scale for Depressive Disorders in Childhood." *Journal of Child Psychology and Psychiatry and Allied Disciplines*, 1987, *28*, 43–60.

Brent, D. A., Kalas, R., Edelbrock, C., Costello, A. J., Dulcan, M., and Conover, N. "Psychopathology and Its Relationship to Suicidal Ideation in Childhood and Adolescents." *Journal of the American Academy of Child and Adolescent Psychiatry*, 1986, *25*, 666–673.

Carlson, G. A., Asarnow, J. R., and Orbach, I. "Developmental Aspects of Suicidal Behavior in Children, Part 1." *Journal of the American Academy of Child and Adolescent Psychiatry*, 1987, *26*, 186–192.

Carlson, G. A., and Cantwell, D. P. "Suicidal Behavior and Depression in Children and Adolescents." *Journal of the American Academy of Child and Adolescent Psychiatry*, 1982, *21*, 361–368.

Chambers, W. J., Puig-Antich, J., Hirsch, M., Paez, P., Ambrosini, P. J., Tabrizi, M. A., and Davies, M. "The Assessment of Affective Disorders in Children and Adolescents by Semi-Structured Interview: Test-Retest Reliability of the K-SADS-P." *Archives of General Psychiatry*, 1985, *42*, 696–702.

Duncan, O. D. "A Socioeconomic Index for all Occupations." In A. J. Reiss, Jr. (ed.), *Occupations and Social Status.* New York: Arno Press, 1977.

Gould, M. S., and Shaffer, D. "The Impact of Suicide in Television Movies: Evidence for Imitation." *New England Journal of Medicine*, 1986, *315*, 690–694.

Hollinger, P. C., and Offer, D. "Sociodemographic, Epidemiologic, and Individual Attributes." In L. Davidson and M. Linnoila (eds.), *Report of the Secretary's Task Force on Youth Suicide.* Vol. 2: *Risk Factors for Youth Suicide.* DHHS Publication No. ADM 89-1622. Washington, D.C.: Government Printing Office, 1989.

Koocher, G. P. "Childhood, Death, and Cognitive Development." *Developmental Psychology*, 1973, *9*, 369–375.

Kovacs, M., and Puig-Antich, J. " 'Major Psychiatric Disorders' as Risk Factors in Youth Suicide." In L. Davidson and M. Linnoila (eds.), *Report of the Secretary's Task Force on Youth Suicide.* Vol. 2: *Risk Factors for Youth Suicide.* DHHS No. ADM 89-1622. Washington, D.C.: Government Printing Office, 1989.

Myers, K. M., Burke, P., and McCauley, F. "Suicidal Behavior by Hospitalized Preadolescent Children on a Psychiatric Unit." *Journal of the American Academy of Child and Adolescent Psychiatry,* 1985, *24,* 474–480.

Orvaschel, H., Puig-Antich, J., Chambers, W., Tabrizi, M. A., and Johnson, R. "Retrospective Assessment of Child Psychopathology with the Kiddie-SADS-E." *Journal of the American Academy of Child and Adolescent Psychiatry,* 1982, *21,* 392–397.

Pfeffer, C. R., Plutchik, R., and Mizruchi, M. S. "Suicidal and Assaultive Behavior in Children: Classification, Measurement, and Interrelations." *American Journal of Psychiatry,* 1983, *140,* 154–157.

Pfeffer, C. R., Solomon, G., Plutchik, R., Mizruchi, M. S., and Weiner, A. "Suicidal Behavior in Latency-Age Psychiatric Inpatients: A Replication and Cross Validation." *Journal of the American Academy of Child and Adolescent Psychiatry,* 1982, *21,* 564–569.

Phillips, D. P., and Carstensen, L. L. "Clustering of Teenage Suicides After Television News Stories About Suicide." *New England Journal of Medicine,* 1986, *315,* 685–689.

Rich, C. L., Young, D., and Fowler, R. C. "San Diego Suicide Study, Part 1: Young Versus Old Subjects." *Archives of General Psychiatry,* 1986, *43,* 578–582.

Schneidman, E. S. "Suicide Among the Gifted." In E. S. Schneidman (ed.), *Suicidology: Contemporary Developments.* Philadelphia: Grune & Statton, 1976.

Schotte, D. E., and Clum, G. A. "Problem-Solving Skills in Suicidal Psychiatric Patients." *Journal of Consulting and Clinical Psychology,* 1987, *55,* 49–54.

Shaffer, D. "Suicide in Childhood and Early Adolescence." *Journal of Child Psychology and Psychiatry and Allied Disciplines,* 1974, *15,* 275–291.

Shaffer, D., and Fisher, P. "The Epidemiology of Suicide in Children and Young Adolescents." *Journal of the American Academy of Child and Adolescent Psychiatry,* 1981, *20,* 545–565.

Weiner, A. S., and Pfeffer, C. R. "Suicidal Status, Depression, and Intellectual Functioning in Preadolescent Psychiatric Inpatients." *Comprehensive Psychiatry,* 1987, *27,* 373–380.

GABRIELLE A. CARLSON *is professor of psychiatry and pediatrics and director of the Division of Child and Adolescent Psychiatry at the State University of New York, Stony Brook.*

JOAN R. ASARNOW *is associate professor of medical psychology and psychiatry at the University of California, Los Angeles.*

ISRAEL ORBACH *is clinical psychologist and chair of the Department of Psychology at Bar-Ilan University in Israel.*

*A significant implication of developmental aspects of suicidal behavior
is that strategies of prevention and intervention are needed in all
phases of the life cycle.*

Developmental Issues in Child and Adolescent Suicide: A Discussion

Cynthia R. Pfeffer

Development is a major, theoretical, clinical, and research concern for the field of child mental health. That the processes involved are complex has challenged efforts to discover the links that maintain developmental continuities and the breakpoints of transition that signal discontinuities. This volume emphasizes the greatly needed integration of clinical and developmental perspectives for an important child and adolescent mental health problem, that of suicidal behavior.

Recognition of the magnitude of the problem of child and adolescent suicidal behavior in the United States was stimulated by the exceptionally high rates of youth suicide in 1977 and by cluster epidemic incidents of adolescent suicide in the early 1980s. Since 1977, the age-specific rates of suicide of fifteen- to twenty-four-year-olds in the United States have remained high. The need to eliminate youth suicide was highlighted in the 1980s by various suicide prevention efforts. Fervent efforts in this direction included massive media activities concerning the problem, news reports pertaining to youth suicidal deaths, national task forces to study the components of this problem, and efforts to counsel high-risk youths within school settings, especially following a youth suicide event. For example, in 1987, a national effort to understand factors precipitating youth suicide and its prevention was begun and the work of a national task force was published in 1989 in the five-volume *Report of the Secretary's Task Force on Youth Suicide* (Alcohol, Drug Abuse, and Mental Health Administration, 1989). That task force's final recommendations were to (1) develop valid data on suicide and attempted suicide, (2) conduct multidisciplinary research to determine and evaluate risk factors for suicide, (3) evaluate the effectiveness and cost of interventions to prevent suicide, (4) support the delivery of suicide prevention services, (5) inform and educate the public and health service providers about current knowledge in the prevention, diagnosis, and treatment of suicide among youth, and (6) involve both the public and private sectors in prevention of youth suicide. Other notable facets regarding youth suicidal behavior gleaned from work in the 1980s were that media attention to this problem may precipitate a short-term increase in rates of youth suicide by means of processes of imitation and identification with idealized characteristics of reported youth suicide victims (Gould and Shaffer, 1986; Hafner and Schmidtke, 1989; Phillips, Carstensen, and Paight, 1989).

Prevention efforts intensified with a focused approach on school curricula to teach youth about warning signs to recognize risk for suicidal behavior and methods to seek help. Evaluation of such programs suggested that they did not accomplish their intended goal of decreasing suicidal behavior and that such programs may have intensified the problem (Shaffer and others, 1990; Spirato and others, 1988; Vieland and others, 1991).

Epidemiological studies reported a birth cohort effect specific to youth suicide (Goldney and Katsikitis, 1983; Klerman, 1989; Murphy and Wetzel, 1980; Solomon and Hellon, 1980). Adolescents and young adults born since World War II were likely to have higher rates of suicide than youths born at an earlier time. The basis of these findings is unknown, although there is speculation that major sociocultural changes since World War II, such as heightened industrialization and greater mobility, account for this type of cohort effect.

Improvements in biotechnical research methodology by the 1990s set the stage for a burgeoning of new investigations into etiological and developmental factors related to suicidal behavior. Functional and structural elements of brain neurophysiology are an important focus in understanding the biological-etiological factors related to suicidal behavior (Mann and Stanley, 1986; Mann, DeMeo, Keilp, and McBride, 1989).

Seminal reports (Asberg, Thoren, and Traskman, 1976; Traskman, Asberg, Bertilsson, and Sjostrant, 1981) that low levels of 5-hydroxyindolacetic acid and its metabolites are associated with risk for suicide stimulated research in utilizing psychopharmacological agents affecting brain serotonin mechanisms to reduce risk for suicidal behavior.

This book highlights important issues of development that add to the scope of knowledge essential to eventually integrating the processes leading to suicidal behavior. A main emphasis of this book is how developmental characteristics are associated with suicidal behavior. Most of the material presented here highlights findings from cross-sectional comparative studies. It brings together the work of investigators who have focused their efforts on processes of cognition and emotion that are affected by level of development and who address the relations of these factors to suicidal behavior.

The importance of developmental factors associated with psychopathology has enjoyed a renaissance, especially regarding recent efforts to apply longitudinal research methodology to the study of childhood psychopathology.

The advantages of longitudinal research is that causal links to psychopathology can be identified and the effects of developmental processes can be delineated. Such causal links are often not unitary but involve additive elements, continuous influences, and discontinuous events. Individual differences, partly determined by developmental variations, account for aspects of how other factors influence outcome and course.

Rutter (1988, p. 1) noted "that very few causal factors invariably lead to the psychopathological outcome. There are individual differences in susceptibility to the risk factor and also protective mechanisms may operate to reduce the risk of a pathological outcome." An individual's course and outcome are not necessarily predictable from knowledge of the individual's characteristics at a specific point in time. For example, Pfeffer and others (1993) reported that in their sample prepubertal children who attempted suicide were at six times greater risk than normal children for a suicide attempt within a six- to eight-year period of follow-up. However, these researchers found that not every prepubertal individual who attempted suicide made a repeat attempt during the course of a circumscribed period of follow-up. Specifically, 32 percent of prepubertal children who attempted suicide reported another suicide attempt during a six- to eight-year follow-up period.

Rutter (1988, p. 2) emphasized an important concept with regard to predicting a future outcome: "Maladaptive outcomes are dependent on whether the early risk experiences are intensified by later maladaptive circumstances or ameliorated by later beneficial experiences." For example, Pfeffer and others (1993) noted that prepubertal suicidal children who had a mood disorder at an initial assessment in a six- to eight-year follow-up study were more than three times at greater risk for a future suicide attempt than were children who did not have a mood disorder at an initial assessment. Furthermore, the presence of a mood disorder within the year preceding a repeat suicide attempt in the six- to eight-year follow-up period increased risk for such a suicide attempt by more than five times. Essentially, these data suggest that prediction of a future suicide attempt is more strongly determined by proximal rather than distal factors.

Development involves the unfolding of multifactorial processes that are integrated and manifest as specific characteristics at a particular age or point in time. The schemas for these processes, although adequately amenable to study in cross-sectional research designs, are best evaluated longitudinally, and especially by means of prospective investigations. Such research may be particularly useful in characterizing attributes involving cognition and perceptions about oneself that may not be easily recalled retrospectively. This book has laid a groundwork for avenues to pursue in understanding attributes related to ego development, self-continuity and identity, cognitive concepts about suicidal behavior, attitudes about and coping with suicidal impulses, developmental factors that impinge on risk for suicidal behavior, self-esteem, competence, and affect expression. Comparative longitudinal studies of children at high risk for suicidal behavior are extremely rare. Studies that incorporate assessment of these factors will be quite helpful in identifying intra-individual characteristics that may mediate risk for suicidal behavior at various stages of development.

While developmental variations in the phenomenology of suicidal behavior are creatively addressed in this book, a most significant implication of these developmental aspects of suicidal behavior is that strategies for prevention and intervention are needed in all phases of the life cycle. Suicidal behavior occurs in people of all ages. It is associated with symptoms of psychiatric disorders, deficits in social support networks, and intense stressful life events (Pfeffer, 1986; Pfeffer and others, 1991, 1993). It may be mediated by dysfunction or immaturity in cognitive capacities, inability to control painful affects or impulses, or complexity of intrapersonal coping styles. The effects of these factors may vary for different people. Developmental influences associated with age or psychophysiological maturity also may mediate the strength of effects of these factors.

These insights suggest that efforts to limit the incidence and prevalence of suicidal behavior must be based on a multifactorial approach that requires consideration of developmental concerns. For example, children are by developmental necessity highly dependent on their parents for nurturance and guidance. A suicidal child who lacks adequate support from parents must be treated with an approach that takes account of ways to amplify adequate parental support by treating parental psychological or medical pathology and family conflicts or by offering substitute resources for family deficiency. While a similar approach applies for adolescents, other social roles are prominent. Problems in peer relations are important risk factors for youth suicidal behavior. Emphasis on fostering better peer group support is a needed component in treating a suicidal adolescent. Other developmental periods also may have specific characteristics of social support systems. The elderly are quite dependent on family or social agency support. Lack of adequacy in these domains may promote serious isolation, physical maladies, and psychological maladjustment. Attention to creating a reasonably consistent interpersonal and home-life support network may reduce factors contributing to suicidal risk in the elderly. Thus, by appreciating the "developmental lines" for social support throughout the life cycle, interventions can be specified to reverse deficits in these developmentally necessary domains.

A cognitive orientation to treatment of suicidal individuals can be planned once developmental characteristics of an individual are known. Deviations from developmental norms must be identified and compensatory adjustments made. Such approaches may focus on amplifying developmentally appropriate coping skills involving interpersonal problem-solving maneuvers, appreciation of hopefulness, and reversal of negative attributions. Such interventions must be programmed to meet the specific developmental capacities of the potentially suicidal individual.

Finally, much is to be learned about aberrations in neurophysiological factors at different developmental periods that are associated with suicidal behavior. The possibilities for limiting these aberrations are heightened by the rapid technological advances in understanding complex brain functions, such as the relationship of deficits in serotonin functioning to suicidal behavior. Suitable psychopharmacological interventions and psychosocial strategies can be applied specifically to decrease the maladaptive outcomes of these biological deficits.

The editors and authors of this book are to be congratulated for integrating clinical and developmental domains with regard to suicidal behavior. Future perspectives can build on this book. One hope is to link efforts of understanding specific areas of biological, cognitive, social, and psychological realms and to decipher their effects, attributes, and outcomes within a developmental perspective for suicidal behavior. An important perspective that will emerge in the 1990s is the impact of development on normal and pathological outcomes. This book leads this perspective with regard to suicidal behavior.

References

Alcohol, Drug Abuse, and Mental Health Administration. *Report of the Secretary's Task Force on Youth Suicide.* DHHS Publication No. ADM 89-1621. Washington, D.C.: Government Printing Office, 1989.

Asberg, M., Thoren, P., and Traskman, L. "Serotonin Depression: A Biochemical Subgroup Within the Affective Disorders?" *Science,* 1976, *191,* 478–480.

Goldney, R. D., and Katsikitis, M. "What Analysis of Suicide Rates in Australia?" *Archives of General Psychiatry,* 1983, *40,* 71–74.

Gould, M. S., and Shaffer, D. "The Impact of Suicide in Television Movies: Evidence for Imitation." *New England Journal of Medicine,* 1986, *315,* 690–694.

Hafner, H., and Schmidtke, A. "Do Televised Fictional Suicide Models Produce Suicides?" In C. R. Pfeffer (ed.), *Suicide Among Youth: Perspectives on Risk and Prevention.* Washington, D.C.: American Psychiatric Press, 1989.

Klerman, G. L. "Suicide, Depression, and Related Problems Among the Baby Boom Cohort." In C. R. Pfeffer (ed.), *Suicide Among Youth: Perspectives on Risk and Prevention.* Washington, D.C.: American Psychiatric Press, 1989.

Mann, J. J., DeMeo, M. D., Keilp, J. G., and McBride, P. A. "Biological Correlates of Suicidal Behavior in Youth." In C. R. Pfeffer (ed.), *Suicide Among Youth: Perspectives on Risk and Prevention.* Washington, D.C.: American Psychiatric Press, 1989.

Mann, J. J., and Stanley, M. *Psychobiology of Suicidal Behavior.* New York: New York Academy of Sciences, 1986.

Murphy, G. E., and Wetzel, R. D. "Suicide Risk by Birth Cohort in the United States." *Archives of General Psychiatry,* 1980, *37,* 519–523.

Pfeffer, C. R. *The Suicidal Child.* New York: Guilford, 1986.

Pfeffer, C. R., Klerman, G. L., Hurt, S. W., Kakuma, T., Peskin, J. R., and Siefker, C. A. "Suicidal Children Grow Up: Rates and Psychosocial Risk Factors for Suicide Attempts During Follow-Up." *Journal of the American Academy of Child and Adolescent Psychiatry,* 1993, *32,* 106–113.

Pfeffer, C. R., Klerman, G. L., Hurt, S. W., Lesser, M., Peskin, J. R., and Siefker, C. A. "Suicidal Children Grow Up: Demographic and Clinical Risk Factors for Adolescent Suicide Attempts." *Journal of the American Academy of Child and Adolescent Psychiatry,* 1991, *30,* 609–616.

Phillips, D. P., Carstensen, L. L., and Paight, D. J. "Effects of Mass Media News Stories on Suicide, with New Evidence on the Role of Story Content." In C. R. Pfeffer (ed.), *Suicide Among Youth: Perspectives on Risk and Prevention.* Washington, D.C.: American Psychiatric Press, 1989.

Rutter, M. *Studies of Psychosocial Risk: The Power of Longitudinal Data.* New York: Cambridge University Press, 1988.

Shaffer, D., Vieland, V., Garland, A., Rojar, M., Underwood, M., and Busner, C. "Adolescent Suicide Attempters: Response to Suicide Prevention." *Journal of the American Medical Association,* 1990, *264,* 3151–3155.

Solomon, M. I., and Hellon, C. P. "Suicide and Age in Alberta, Canada, 1951–1977." *Archives of General Psychiatry,* 1980, *37,* 511–513.

Spirato, A., Overholser, J., Ashworth, S., Morgan, J., and Benedict-Drew, C. "Evaluations of a Suicide Awareness Curriculum for High School Students." *Journal of the American Academy of Child and Adolescent Psychiatry,* 1988, *27,* 705–711.

Traskman, L., Asberg, M., Bertilsson, L., and Sjostrant, L. "Monoamine Metabolites in CSF and Suicidal Behavior." *Archives of General Psychiatry,* 1981, *38,* 631–636.

Vieland, V., Whittle, B., Garland, A., Hicks, R., and Shaffer, D. "The Impact of Curriculum-Based Suicide Prevention Programs for Teenagers: An Eighteen-Month Follow-Up." *Journal of the American Academy of Child and Adolescent Psychiatry,* 1991, *30,* 811–815.

CYNTHIA R. PFEFFER is professor of psychiatry at Cornell University Medical College and chief of the Child Psychiatry Inpatient Unit at New York Hospital, Westchester Division.

INDEX

Ordering Information

New Directions for Child Development is a series of paperback books that presents the latest research findings on all aspects of children's psychological development, including their cognitive, social, moral, and emotional growth. Books in the series are published quarterly in Fall, Winter, Spring, and Summer and are available for purchase by subscription and individually.

Subscriptions for 1994 cost $54.00 for individuals (a savings of 25 percent over single-copy prices) and $75.00 for institutions, agencies, and libraries. Please do not send institutional checks for personal subscriptions. Standing orders are accepted.

Single copies cost $17.95 when payment accompanies order. (California, New Jersey, New York, and Washington, D.C., residents please include appropriate sales tax.) All orders will be charged postage and handling.

Discounts for quantity orders are available. Please write to the address below for information.

All orders must include either the name of an individual or an official purchase order number. Please submit your order as follows:
    Subscriptions: specify series and year subscription is to begin
    Single copies: include individual title code (such as CD59)

Mail all orders to:
    Jossey-Bass Publishers
    350 Sansome Street
    San Francisco, California 94104-1342

For subscription sales outside of the United States, contact any international subscription agency or Jossey-Bass directly.

OTHER TITLES AVAILABLE IN THE
NEW DIRECTIONS FOR CHILD DEVELOPMENT SERIES
William Damon, Editor-in-Chief